the intellectual

the intellectual

steve fuller

ICON BOOKS

Published in the UK in 2005 by Icon Books Ltd,
The Old Dairy, Brook Road, Thriplow, Cambridge SG8 7RG
e-mail: info@iconbooks.co.uk
www.iconbooks.co.uk

Sold in the UK, Europe, South Africa and Asia
by Faber and Faber Ltd, 3 Queen Square,
London WC1N 3AU
or their agents

Distributed in the UK, Europe, South Africa and Asia
by TBS Ltd, Frating Distribution Centre, Colchester Road,
Frating Green, Colchester CO7 7DW

Published in Australia in 2005
by Allen & Unwin Pty Ltd,
PO Box 8500, 83 Alexander Street,
Crows Nest, NSW 2065

Distributed in Canada by
Penguin Books Canada,
10 Alcorn Avenue, Suite 300,
Toronto, Ontario M4V 3B2

ISBN 1 84046 653 7

Typesetting by Hands Fotoset

Printed and bound in the UK by
Mackays of Chatham

CONTENTS

INTRODUCTION

The text before you is modelled loosely on Machiavelli's *The Prince*, the notorious 16th-century book of advice on how to govern. The source of *The Prince*'s notoriety is the single-mindedness with which Machiavelli pursued his topic: everything – from intimate relations to religious rituals – is judged in terms of its ability to acquire and maintain power. Machiavelli wrote this way because he wanted the book to serve as a demonstration of his own worth for employment in a princely court. By that standard the book failed abysmally, placing Machiavelli under constant suspicion, and sometimes arrest, for the rest of his days.

However, Machiavelli was a very successful intellectual and deserves to be honoured as such. He said what everyone knew but refused to acknowledge. He spoke truth to power, when power was not accustomed to being addressed in that fashion. Like most intellectuals, Machiavelli stood for an ideal that had little chance of being realised in his lifetime – in his case, Roman civic republicanism. However, like all intellectuals, he developed his viewpoint in terms of the politics of his day, which centred on volatile city-states ruled by ambitious dynasties. This odd juxtaposition of the ideal and the real has led to no end of confusion about the 'spirit' in which Machiavelli's advice was supposed to be taken: again, a fate shared by many intellectuals.

My book is for and about people like Machiavelli. I write as an intellectual in academia, which increasingly looks like a state of exile from the intellectual world. Historically the university has been the breeding ground of intellectuals. In particular, the introduction of tenured professorships in the 19th century provided aspiring intellectuals with the opportunity – too bad not the obligation – to pursue lines of inquiry with impunity, challenging the received wisdom in one's chosen field. At the dawn of the 21st century, this aspect of academic life seems to be in terminal decline. Unfortunately, there is little sense of what is being lost in the process. *The Intellectual* aims to provide a vivid sense of the virtue that is 'intellectual autonomy', and a justification of its preservation and encouragement by whatever institutional means are available.

This book has a tripartite structure, which is designed to get at many of the same themes from somewhat different angles. The first part consists of four short essays that define some key characteristics of the intellectual, drawing on both historical and contemporary examples. Since the intellectual is a somewhat elusive figure, all too often seen through the eyes of opponents, much of the book is devoted to distinguishing the intellectual from

such related characters as the ideologue, the entrepreneur, the marketer, the journalist, the lawyer, the
academic and the scientist. But clearly, the intellectual's
closest and more troublesome kin is the philosopher.
Thus, the second part is an extended dialogue between
an intellectual and a philosopher. The third and final part
consists of a set of frequently asked questions about
intellectuals. The book concludes with a brief list of
works that figured in the composition of my argument.

The impatient reader may already want to know some
basic tips on how to be an intellectual. Based on my own
experience, I would offer five pieces of advice that will
reappear with greater elaboration and justification in the
pages that follow.

First, learn to see things from multiple points of view
without losing your ability to evaluate them. Always
imagine that at some point you will need to make a
decision about what to believe of these different perspectives. Second, be willing and able to convey any thought
in any medium. There would be little point in being an
intellectual if you did not believe that ideas, in some
sense, always transcend their mode of communication.
Third, never regard a point of view as completely false or
beneath contempt. There is plenty of truth and error to
go around, and you can never really be sure which is
which. Fourth, always see your opinion as counter-
balancing, rather than reinforcing, someone else's
opinion. Fifth, in public debate fight for the truth
tenaciously but concede error graciously.

I would also like to offer a word of advice to academics: even if you have personally lost the urge to be an intellectual, you are nevertheless seeding the next generation of intellectuals. Resist the temptation to quash the free-ranging and often reckless spirit that marks the first flowering of the critical intellect. It is too easy to invoke rules and standards that you know – and in other contexts would admit – are arbitrarily imposed for the sake of administrative convenience. If you cannot honestly justify academic strictures on intellectual grounds, then be as open as possible about the power relations that compel you to restrict or censure the student's mode of expression. It is natural for students to be confused about many things, but they should never leave your office confused on this matter. Academics are of course entitled to believe that the sort of intellectual defended in these pages is unsustainable. Indeed, such a belief may help you rationalise your own career. But it is merely a belief, not a proof. In the end, the concept of academic freedom is twofold: it upholds not only the freedom to teach but also the freedom to learn. Intel-lectuals are bred when the *student's* academic freedom is treated with respect.

Research and teaching across different disciplines provides ideal academic training for the intellectual. My own career, centred on developing the research programme of 'social epistemology', is very much of this character. Social epistemology is concerned with how knowledge should be produced, in light of what is known about how it has been produced. In effect, it is a kind of abstract science policy. Each discipline has much to contribute to this project, though these contributions are likely to be valued more highly outside than inside a given discipline. This is because insights about the social character of knowledge often betray the secrets of cross-disciplinary power struggles that both stronger and weaker parties, for complementary reasons, would rather leave concealed. In that respect, the social epistemologist is a trainee intellectual who speaks truth to power in the localised setting of the university. The university does not constitute the entire universe of public discourse – but it provides a good platform to go further.

Also on the topic of location, it is worth saying that although the British like to portray themselves as 'anti-intellectual', the UK is very likely the most intellectual nation in the English-speaking world, judged in terms of the quantity and quality of its academic and mass intellectual media. (I write as a US citizen who has been resident in the UK for the past ten years.) With that in mind, I want to thank Simon Flynn for enabling me to write this book for Icon, and Duncan Heath for his expert editing. In recent years, I have also benefited from speaking at some distinctive public forums in this country, including the Café Scientifique and the Bath Royal Literary and Scientific Institution. I want to thank Duncan Dallas and Victor Suchar for helping to main-tain a live public intellectual culture. Over the past decade, I have been able to participate in debates sponsored by the *Times Higher Education Supplement*, the *New Scientist* and the *Independent*. In addition, I would like to draw attention to an intriguing experiment in the creation of a global public intellectual culture to which I have had the privilege to contribute, the Prague-based 'Project Syndicate' (www.project-syndicate.org). In all these settings, alongside the more than 500 public lectures I have delivered around the world over the past two decades, I have learned that, yes, any idea worth thinking can be conveyed at any length to any audience. Never confuse the laziness or impatience of élites with the depth of their ideas.

Other individuals have influenced and inspired me as I tried to get a grip on this topic: Stephen Toulmin, Phil Mirowski, Zia Sardar, Nico Stehr, Charles Turner, Joan Leach, Jim Collier, Bill Lynch, Bill Keith, Sujatha Raman, Babette Babich, Merle Jacob, Thoms Hellström, James Mittra, Hugo Mendes, Thomas Basbøll, Aditi Gowri, Jenna Hartel, Gene Rosa, Alf Bång, Jeremy Shearmur and Libby Schweber. As the years go by, I also find my original graduate training at the University of Pittsburgh, in both history and philosophy of science and rhetoric, of unexpected value. Thanks here to Ted McGuire, Charlie Willard and John Poulakos. Finally, I must apologise to my long-suffering students whose papers I delayed marking to finish this book, and last but not least my long-suffering partner, Stephanie Lawler.

Coventry, England
June 2004

Four Theses
on Intellectuals

1. Intellectuals Were Born on the Back Foot

The intellectual is a philosopher without the benefit of Plato's spin

The clearest sign that historical judgements are hard to reverse is the fate of specific groups whose names come to stand for vices and liabilities in humanity at large: 'Huns' and 'Vandals', 'anarchists' and 'fascists' come to mind. For the intellectual, the relevant group in this category are the *sophists*, the great pretenders to reason in ancient Athens. Most intellectuals would take the characterisation of their activities as 'sophistic' to be an insult, or at least a challenge to the integrity of their thought. Nevertheless, the sophists were the original intellectuals and continue to have much of value to teach the budding intellectual – that is, once we give a more balanced account of their activities.

Not surprisingly, the sophists have been largely defined by their opponents. The sophists are known mainly as the people who figure in Plato's dialogues as

Socrates' cleverest foils. Several of the dialogues bear the names of the most eminent sophists, such as Protagoras and Gorgias. In ancient Greek, 'sophists' was simply a generic term for 'wise men', but once Plato got hold of the word, it came to stand for the original *wise guys*, arrogant bluffers who fail to match the depth of a genuine philosopher like Socrates. Of course, thanks to his devoted student Plato, Socrates lives on as the icon of Western critical rationalism. Rehabilitating the sophists today is bound to be an uphill struggle.

Nevertheless, to the average Athenian citizen, circa 400 BC, there was not much to choose between Socrates and the sophists. They all spent their days arguing about everything under the sun, each trying to outdo the other in the logical knots from which he would escape. They attracted fans in the rest of the population, typically among impressionable rich young men, who would fuel the dialectics with food and drink. Every now and then, some of these young men would get the opportunity to apply what they had heard, often resulting in reckless policies with disastrous consequences.

However, in one significant respect, the sophists differed from Socrates. Socrates was an Athenian citizen whose endless talk was a form of leisure subsidised by a military pension and an inherited estate. In contrast, the sophists were foreign merchants for whom sparring with Socrates was an 'infomercial' for verbal skills that could be imparted to anyone who could afford the sophists' going rate. To the untutored Athenian eye, there was nothing especially strange about the interaction between Socrates and these merchants: the wealthy Athenians were notoriously tough customers when faced with traders trying to oversell their wares. The subtle difference was that Socrates haggled over the very existence of the goods the sophists claimed to supply.

So what did the sophists have to sell? Not ideas exactly. To be sure, Socrates regarded ideas as the currency of thought. But he regarded them as the property of the gods. The gods might share their ideas with us once we are in the right frame of mind, but ideas cannot be bought and sold at will. Yet the sophists never spoke of themselves as 'idea merchants', as one might characterise think-tank dwellers today or, in more elevated tones, Erasmus, Voltaire or Bertrand Russell, each of whom made a decent living from opening up people's minds.

No, the sophists were purveyors of certain skills and perhaps even tools. Perhaps these skills and tools – what Plato demonised as 'rhetoric' – could be used to *forge* ideas. It was just this sacrilegious possibility that Socrates made vivid to his audience: that is, to try to make for oneself what only the gods could bestow. But the sophists mainly wanted to help clients win lawsuits and sway public opinion, to take greater control of their fate, as befits citizens in a democracy. In today's world, the sophists would be most at home running management training seminars and writing self-help books. A latter-day Socrates might then stigmatise these people as 'gurus' and complain about their works jostling for space

9

in the college curriculum and the 'philosophy' section of bookshops.

It is worth dwelling on the curious indifference with which the sophists ultimately regarded the kind of ideas Socrates upheld. For them, an idea is only as good as the action it permits. Depending on the context, your best course of action may be to stick with conventional ideas; on other occasions, inventiveness may better serve you. The sophist's speciality was in judging the marginal difference between alternative strategies. However, such a capacity for discrimination requires clarity of purpose, for which one takes personal responsibility. An important sophistic lesson is that people typically commit errors in thought and action because they lack a clear sense of what they want, and hence cannot decide on a suitable means for achieving it. When Protagoras famously uttered, 'Man is the measure of all things', he meant that we ultimately set the standard by which we would have others judge us.

However, Socrates twisted this striking assertion of intellectual autonomy into an admission of impiety, since the sophists believed that even the gods are only as good as the actions permitted by invoking their names. Did this not mean that the sophists would have each citizen become his own god – a law unto himself? And would that not bring chaos to the city-state? Socrates certainly did all he could to convert this chain of leading questions into a self-fulfilling prophecy. Some claim that the frenzy Socrates stirred up about the teachings of

Protagoras in particular led to the burning of his books upon his death, which began the tradition of the sophists being known exclusively through the eyes of their opponents.

Perhaps the most influential of these anti-sophists, Plato's student Aristotle, flourished just as the sophists were conveniently disappearing from Athens. Aristotle is responsible for attributing to Protagoras his most notorious 'sophism' – now a general term for a fallacious argument strategy: *Since there are two sides to any argument, the weaker argument can always be made to appear the stronger.* Instead of giving this strategy its due as the source of the judicial idea of 'reasonable doubt', Aristotle left the impression that Protagoras was calling for the mishandling of evidence. Seen in a more sympathetic light, however, the Protagorean sophism captures beautifully the intellectual's turn of mind.

First of all, people are inclined to believe the evidence put before them. However, such evidence is subject to the circumstances under which it was collected. For example, one side in a case may have had more financial and rhetorical resources at its disposal than the other. Justice depends on these two opposing tendencies cancelling – *not reinforcing* – each other. Thus, one must always presume that the better-evidenced side merely *appears* better. Given the opportunity, the other side might well have balanced the ledger or even turned out superior.

This line of reasoning implies, among other things, that the evidence relevant to deciding a case is never

11

complete, and hence the judge must always think of herself as taking partial responsibility for its outcome. She acts out of what the Jesuits called 'moral certainty'. In this respect, the judge is not merely an impartial reporter but a direct participant in what constitutes the truth of the case. In this frame of mind, the judge is likely to be less cowed by the usual stamps of authority and more open to the play of possibilities that may be relevant to the case but, for contingent reasons, have not been so far evidenced in it.

The sophistic approach to justice never ceases to be controversial. An interesting recent example is a book written in the wake of the 11 September 2001 bombing of New York's World Trade Center, *After the Terror* by the philosopher Ted Honderich. It argues, among other things, that the Palestinians are entitled to their terrorist activities, if we condone the kinds of actions taken by the Israeli government to secure its borders. Honderich does not himself endorse terrorism, but equally he does not believe that we do justice to those who pursue it, if we don't judge the activity in a principled fashion: if terrorism is already implicitly permissible in some forms, then why not permit all forms openly? Would it not be a greater injustice to sanction only some select groups of terrorists simply because they combine just the right amounts of annoyance and weakness? However these questions are answered, we are left with the prospect of having to revise radically our attitude towards at least particular terrorists, and maybe even terrorism as such.

I deliberately picked Honderich because he published *After the Terror* just as he was retiring from the Grote Chair in the Philosophy of Mind and Logic at University College London. Honderich's own philosophical pro-clivities – an aggressive mix of materialism, determinism and democratic socialism – mark him as a latter-day sophist. But the name behind his chair makes the connection still tighter. George Grote was a City banker and Liberal MP, who in his spare time had mastered sufficient Greek to spearhead a revival of the sophists in the Victorian era. Grote's sophists were the intellectual ancestors of his political allies, utilitarian philosophers like Jeremy Bentham and John Stuart Mill. Indeed, learning from the sophists' own fate, the utilitarians ensured that their legacy would not disappear with their deaths. Thus, they secured financial backing for founding the University of London as an academy for religious dissenters and other fee-paying outsiders to the Oxbridge establishment.

Unfortunately, thanks to Plato, one of the impression-able rich young men who sat at Socrates' feet, the sophists have now been largely in disrepute for almost 2,500 years. However, as might be expected, Plato's story is spun. We are used to thinking about Socrates as having driven the sophists from the forum in Athens, just as Jesus would later drive the merchants – the 'money changers' – from the temple in Jerusalem. Both episodes are normally seen as acts of *purification* that returned reason to its roots. However, in their own day, they were seen as acts of *exaggeration* that took reason beyond its self-defined bounds. Why else would both Socrates and Jesus have been eventually condemned to death by their peers? (One measure of human progress is a society's capacity to extract wisdom from such expressive excess peacefully: in short, to absorb the message without literally killing the messenger. When intellectuals long for utopia, this is it.)

To the Athenian court that put him to death, citizen Socrates should have known better and not encouraged the sophists in their worst tendencies. After all, the sophists were only trying to make a living by providing Athens with skills that, for the most part, were of genuine use. There was no need for Socrates to have baited the sophists, who as foreigners were only made defensive, causing them to redouble their claims in ways that would invite a polarisation of Athens between those who trusted and distrusted the sophists' powers. Such a climate of hyperbole was largely responsible for the volatile policy environment that made the city-state vulnerable to its enemies.

But Plato put a different spin on his mentor's words and deeds. Socrates' refusal to take fees was made into a mark of sanctity, not solvency. His class snobbery towards the sophists' willingness to train anyone at the going rate became an argument for the postulation of capacities – indeed, 'virtues' – whose realisation depends more on possessing the right frame of mind in the first place than any specific form of instruction. Moreover, Socrates' latent xenophobia was spun as a justified

14

suspicion about selling things that people either already owned or could not be sold.

In particular, Socrates denigrated Protagoras' introduction of writing as an *aide-memoire* for delivering speeches. This innovation had enabled Protagoras to develop the first grammar for the Greek language, the founding moment in the history of linguistics. Nevertheless, Socrates managed to portray Protagoras as alienating his clients from their innate linguistic capacity, only to reacquaint them with it at a price. This framing of the sophistic exchange would be used periodically to stigmatise the value placed on theoretical abstraction by Christendom's own outsiders, the Jews. The different attitudes towards writing expressed by Socrates and Protagoras illustrate the ability of intellectuals to see quite different things – of equally momentous import – in the slightest of technical innovations.

Socrates voiced the standard Athenian prejudices to writing, which launched a pincer attack on the practice. On the one hand, the keeping of notes revealed either the feebleness or the insincerity of a speaker whose integrity was tied to the appearance of having direct access to his own thoughts. On the other hand, the best known use of writing at the time was the Egyptian and Near Eastern custom of posting imperial dicta on newsboards, which effectively used language to assert a command structure that severely limited both interpersonal negotiation and public accountability. Either way, the unique kind of alienation bred by writing did not suit the free citizen.

Protagoras argued that, on the contrary, writing established an independent basis for testimony against which speech might be judged, a standard that was not completely beholden to the vagaries of a person's 'trustworthiness' as a witness. As someone who earned a living from teaching people how to appear trustworthy, Protagoras spoke with the authority of a smuggler of illegal aliens who proposed identity cards as the solution to the problem he had helped to create. In other words, there was the question of Protagoras' own trustworthiness: when does sincerely presented relevant experience veer into deceptive special pleading?

Clearly Protagoras stood to benefit as a freelance literary consultant, but still he might also be correct that the doubts writing cast on the instant veracity of speech would open up the sphere of public accountability. At the same time, it was not clear that Socrates, as a respected citizen of Athens, would welcome the added scrutiny to his words: where would the scrutiny end? Is no one's word a sacred trust? If a newly established cult of writing did not succeed in transforming Athens into an authoritarian regime, the wanton proliferation of the skill would enshrine ephemera and make it harder to decide whom to believe.

The culture clash between Socrates and Protagoras over the significance of writing has a contemporary ring: at least it resonates with the 1980s. Socratic fears over the dissemination of writing anticipate the intellectual who distrusts thinking on a computer, pointing to the irresponsibility of impersonal data transmission, the impending information explosion and the consequent end to quality control – not to mention the increased surveillance capacities afforded to both Big Brother and Big Business. From that standpoint, Protagoras' defence of writing looks like the early visionary statements of intellectual liberation that would be offered by personal computers in a world previously acquainted only with massive mainframes.

Of course, both the hopes of Protagoras and the fears of Socrates came to be realised. And the same may be said of the parallel discussion that occurred about computers over 2,000 years later. More importantly, for our purposes, Protagoras and Socrates provide two complementary styles of being an intellectual. Both ultimately involve chasing ideas that are, in some sense, detachable from their material containers. Thus, for Protagoras, writing was more than simply the sum of the dubious uses to which it had already been put – it was a potential waiting to be exploited in new and typically counter-intuitive directions. Socrates saw matters quite in reverse: writing was a temptation that in the guise of novelty concealed age-old problems and pitfalls that had to be anticipated and disclosed to prevent his society from doing something it would later regret.

These two images of the intellectual – half prospector, half inquisitor – have co-existed uneasily over the centuries. As an exercise in self-presentation, the history of philosophy has been largely devoted to demonising and marginalising the extreme versions of both types. True philosophers avoid both the entrepreneurial optimism encouraged by Protagoras and the paranoid pessimism to which Socrates could be prone. Those who don't manage to navigate between these two extremes are consigned to the ranks of 'mere intellectuals'.

Needless to say, Socrates had the last laugh in all this. Plato was sufficiently impressed by Protagorean arguments for the long-term significance of writing that he made a point of immortalising his own master in a series of dialogues that remain the most consistently well-written body of work in the Western philosophical canon. This was how 'sophist' came to stand for the bundle of qualities displayed by *both* protagonists, Protagoras and Socrates, at their most distinctive. To understand what it is to be an intellectual is to learn to embrace this distinctiveness, once again.

2. Intellectuals Are Touched by Paranoia

Paranoia is the pathological version of the intellectual's normal frame of mind

The paranoid personality suffers from a persecution complex born of megalomania, the sort of 'big-headedness' that normally leads the intellectual to exaggerate her own significance. The paranoid sees herself as a reliable instrument – perhaps even a microcosm – of the overall state of reality. The paranoid's experience provides evidence for a grand conspiracy. Moreover, the perpetrators know that she is on to their ruse, which maintains its hold only through the mass ignorance of its victims. Once the ruse is revealed in all its ramifications, the conspirators' power will immediately dissolve. Thus, the paranoid reasons, the conspirators do everything they can to throw her off the trail by planting false or deceptive leads and rendering their victims unwitting accomplices in their ruses. Any revelation of the conspiracy is therefore bound to be inconclusive, always in need of further investigation, as the conspirators resort to still more clever and complex ruses. The longer the chase continues, the more the paranoid realises her quarry is really a body snatcher capable of assuming many human forms. Indeed, the conspiracy is nothing but an *idea*.

A conspiracy theory is a kind of social scientific hypothesis. It says that a relatively tight-knit group of people – most of them hidden from public view – are responsible for a rather large and diffuse social phenomenon. Sometimes conspiracy theories happen to be true. However, they are often false because the world turns out to be more complicated than the conspiracy theorist admits. A good way to counter a conspiracy theory is to say that the phenomenon it's supposed to explain would have happened anyway, by some other means, even without the alleged conspirators.

But this rebuttal had better not work all the time. Otherwise, it would be impossible to hold anyone responsible for anything. Not only would the intellectual's borderline paranoia be undermined, but so too would the normal means of bringing people to justice. It would also invalidate the positive version of conspiracy theorising, *social engineering*, whereby certain desired outcomes are produced according to plan. In short, at stake in admitting at least the occasional validity of conspiracy theories is the efficacy of human reason on a large scale – for *both* good and ill. Because intellectuals believe in the concerted power of reason to change the world, they are always looking – even hoping – for conspiracies.

The worst course of action for an intellectual faced with a conspiracy theory is to ignore it, lest she be seen as having confessed her own collusion. The next worst move is to suppress the conspiracy theory. This would only redouble the efforts of the theory's supporters, as suppression would constitute recognition of the threat they pose to the status quo. The intellectual's best strategy is simply to take the conspiracy theory at face value and give it a full public airing, no matter how politically incorrect its claims might be: treat the conspiracy theorist for what she is, a fellow intellectual.

A sure test of an intellectual's commitment to the Enlightenment motto, 'The truth shall set you free', is a willingness to debate even the most taboo of subjects. There are no 'dark sides' to any ideas, except the light that fails to be shed on them. Unlike scientists and other experts, the intellectual has sufficient faith in human reason – fallible as it is – to want to encourage people to judge even highly contested matters for themselves. If, as experts often believe, people tend to confuse the true and the false, then that may simply show that so-called truths are conjectures whose refutations have been institutionally delayed.

The modern world is marked by the ease with which taboo topics can be generated from the interface of scientific research and public policy. Two persistently tabooed hypotheses that attract conspiracy theories are (1) that intelligence is unequally distributed among biologically salient subgroups of humans (especially 'races') and (2) that the pattern of life in the universe strongly implies a cosmic design. According to the conspiracy theorists, such hypotheses are not evaluated fairly. They are held to a higher than normal standard of proof, if not dismissed out of hand; their attempts to rethink what counts as evidence are miscast as the sheer denial of evidence; and so on.

But what is the nature of the conspiracy that has rendered these hypotheses taboo? In brief, the scientific establishment is in collusion with what remains of the welfare state, and so any line of research likely to challenge its egalitarian and secular premises is ruled out of bounds. Faced with these charges, how should the intellectual respond? Answer: call the conspirators' bluff.

There is certainly prima facie evidence from outside

the conspirators' quarters that the peer review processes of science constitute an 'old boys' network' that is biased against unorthodox views put forward by strange people from out-of-the-way places. Moreover, as Thomas Kuhn correctly observed, science maintains the clarity of its research frontier, its forward momentum, by evaluating research solely in terms of its potential contribution to the dominant paradigm. Ideas, proposals and even findings that explicitly try to change the subject or overturn the paradigm are thus rarely welcomed.

So the conspirators appear to have a point, despite manifold attempts by philosophical defenders of science – not least Kuhn himself – to justify a paradigm's sophisticated but systematic form of censorship as the best of all possible worlds of organised inquiry. Such attempts strike the intellectual as sheer hypocrisy, akin to the commissar who disallows free speech for a large segment of the population because of what she anticipates to be their subversive messages.

But hypocrisy abounds in this debate. The conspirators complaining about their marginalisation from the scientific mainstream do not themselves lack support. Indeed, their demonisation as 'racists' and 'Creationists' suggests they are a genuine threat to the scientific establishment. How is that possible, if they are so marginal? Obviously there are alternative sources of support for science in society, each of which would pull it in a somewhat different direction. The so-called peer review process is typically used by professional scientific bodies, through which the state tends to fund science. However, these bodies do not exhaust science's full constituency. There are many private foundations – rooted in business, religion or both – that have an interest in betting against the scientific orthodoxy in the long run, especially given the post-Cold-War tendency for states to devolve their control over research budgets.

Until recently, science has operated as a state-protected market. But now science is undergoing a shift from being an agent of secularisation to itself being secularised. Those who recoil at the prospect are like 16th-century Catholics who had to be reminded that Protestants are not atheists. Proponents of 'genetic diversity' and 'intelligent design' – the scientifically updated and politically correct terms for 'racism' and 'Creationism' – do not oppose or violate science. They do not even claim to be advancing 'alternative' sciences. They simply want to take the same scientific legacy into a different future.

So where does this leave us? Yes, there probably is a conspiracy to render certain topics taboo from science and public policy. But no, the conspiracy does not matter much because taboos surrounding, say, racism and Creationism can be evaded with relative ease. However, what neither side wishes to discuss is that the future of science is under-determined by its past.

Neo-Darwinian biology can take us into a racist or a non-racist future, depending on how we decide to use the theory. Similarly, cosmology can take us into a theist or non-theist future. The histories of both disciplines provide precedents for going in either direction. Moreover, supporters of research in both fields already implicitly know this. It would be difficult to motivate the continuing and intensifying interest in either Darwinism or cosmology, if supporters did not think that impending discoveries would vindicate their moral and political preferences. An enduring lesson of the modern world is that the subtlest means of imposing radical political solutions is to demonstrate the backing of science. Now that's a form of paranoia worth nursing.

Generally speaking, a good test for an intellectual's paranoid tendencies is her steadfast belief that there is something profoundly right about the Marxist theory of capitalist exploitation. Even if the domestic economy appears to improve from deregulated markets, it is probably at the expense of exploitation overseas. Whenever a wrong is done, someone is to blame: the more tolerable the wrong, the more extensive the culpability. Bystanders to wrongdoing can always find it in their self-interest to remain silent, and over time the significance of their cowardice may evaporate as memories fade of who was at the scene of the crime. Indeed, if intellectuals were inclined to believe in Original Sin, this would be its mark: that people can routinely get away with, and even benefit from, keeping their counsel, refusing either to examine the evidence for themselves or, worse, to declare what they truly believe to be the case. If you're an intellectual, 'tact' is the tactful way of referring to cowardice.

In partial remedy of human frailty, the intellectual might follow the trail that eventuates in the evil deed. Her quarry is an elusive inequality of power and resources – or, if *au fait* with the latest in economics and psychology, she might seek to divine the 'information asymmetries' that stabilise social systems in ways that regularly disadvantage certain parties and silence those in a position to tell about it. Of course, the intellectual expects to be thrown off the trail by the sort of *post hoc* rationalisations that led Marxists to turn 'ideology' into a pejorative word. The more sophisticated the rationalisation offered for patently sub-optimal circumstances, the more evil there is to hide. If something that strikes you as bad is presented as better than all the alternatives, then you know evil is afoot because you are effectively being discouraged from asking how things got so bad in the first place. 'Invisible hand' explanations, whereby private vices allegedly make for public virtue, tend to induce precisely this diabolical form of distraction.

As it turns out, paranoia also captures the state of mind responsible for launching the history of modern philosophy. In the 17th century, René Descartes insisted that without a foundation of indubitable principles, our knowledge might just as well be an elaborate ruse generated by an evil demon. Descartes himself famously proposed a set of such principles, beginning with *Cogito ergo sum*: 'I think therefore I am.' Thereafter Descartes was interpreted as having solved the *problem* of scepticism, which, in the fine tradition of paranoid intellectuals, was a figment of his imagination.

Before Descartes, scepticism had been considered a solution – not a problem. The original sceptics of ancient Greece were the West's own Buddhists. They devised an ethic for a world where the True and the False can never be distinguished with certainty. They cultivated a higher indifference, which in practice amounted to supreme tolerance. The perennial character of this attitude should not be underestimated. Its most celebrated modern exemplar, Michel de Montaigne, died only a few years before Descartes was born. However, Christian doctrine left a more lasting impression on Descartes. For him, scepticism was not a source of equanimity but a moral risk, our potential hostage to evil. Descartes fretted over the unfortunate consequences likely to befall those who fail to recognise the divine guarantor of the True. Whereas Greek paganism had encouraged humans to blend in with the rest of nature, Christianity saw the world in more polarised terms, urging the faithful to resist the call of nature. Thus, scepticism became a cause for urgency rather than a source of relief.

The intellectual secularises the Cartesian vision of scepticism by producing what Stalin's house intellectual, György Lukács, called *oppositional consciousness*. As long as reason remains unequally exercised across humanity, the intellectual will oppose what most people appear to believe because they are likely to be under the thumb of a dominant power. Such a superior attitude

26

towards popular opinion certainly evokes the paranoid's megalomania. But how does it square with the intellectual's democratic sentiment that people can decide for themselves?

For a start, most people rarely *decide* to believe anything in particular, simply because it is more convenient to move through a world already equipped with default beliefs. Active rejection takes work, passive acceptance does not. The intellectual ennobles humanity by providing opportunities for resistance – that is, situations that force us to take decisions. Put more mundanely, by exercising oppositional consciousness, the intellectual behaves like a consumer who refuses to buy off the shelf. Not surprisingly, consumer collectives display many of the key characteristics of intellectuals writ large. They judge goods by the nature of their producers and the availability of alternatives. Like the discriminating consumer, the intellectual is suspicious of ideas monopolised by a producer with a dubious track record. Such ideas constitute what the Italian Marxist Antonio Gramsci called a 'hegemony'.

The first time Cartesian urgency was expressed as a general sensibility – one that would come to characterise the modern intellectual – occurred a century after Descartes' death, in response to the great Lisbon earthquake on All Saints' Day, 1755. Theologians claimed that divine justice was somehow served by the loss of 30,000 lives and the destruction of 9,000 buildings. This response was ridiculed as 'the best of all possible worlds' by Voltaire, the greatest intellectual of the day, in his novel *Candide*. He believed instead that the catastrophe merely demonstrated nature's indifference to humanity. The two opposed explanations shared a sense of human powerlessness: there was no specific course of action that the citizens of Lisbon could have taken to avoid the catastrophe. To be sure, Voltaire did not believe that the hubris of Original Sin was the source of the problem, yet he could not hold the Lisboans personally responsible for their fate. In this respect, Voltaire thought very much like a Greek sceptic.

Nevertheless, Voltaire came under attack by fellow Enlightenment wit Jean-Jacques Rousseau, who spoke as an ecologist might today. Rousseau argued that the citizens of Lisbon could have avoided their fate, had they been more mindful of the limits that the environment placed on their actions. Instead they let arrogance and greed cloud their judgement. They overbuilt, and the earthquake demonstrated the error of this strategy. According to Rousseau, the Lisboans had only themselves to blame for permitting the disaster to occur.

Although Rousseau's response appeared unduly harsh in his day, it provided the first clear statement of *vigilance* as a virtue required of intellectuals. Things do not happen simply by accident or for reasons beyond our control. Even things we do not intend may still be anticipated, and the more we can anticipate, the more for which we may then be held responsible. If judges and lawyers are mainly concerned with assigning responsibility for the *commission of specific acts*, intellectuals devote themselves to the second-order task of assigning responsibility for the *permission of types of acts*. In ethics, this locus of concern is called *negative responsibility* — that is, responsibility for what one does not do but could have done. By the end of the 18th century, a quote apocryphally attributed to the Whig politician Edmund Burke begins to epitomise this heightened sense of vigilance: 'All that is necessary for evil to triumph is for good men to do nothing.'

The burden of negative responsibility weighs more heavily on the knowledgeable and the powerful. From the standpoint of the Enlightenment, the advancement of science raises the standard of moral progress, which in turn provides more opportunities for failures of negative responsibility. Thus, levels of human misery that were regrettable but excusable in the 18th and 19th centuries become intolerable and culpable in the 20th and 21st centuries.

Moreover, significant failures of negative responsibility can arise simply from the failure to ask questions, perhaps out of fear of what the answers might reveal. Adolf Eichmann was the Nazi bureaucrat who coordinated the transport of Jews from Germany to the concentration camps in the Second World War. Yet, under examination from an Israeli war crimes tribunal in 1962, he persistently claimed that he was simply following orders from the Nazi high command and held no personal animosity towards the Jews. Eichmann was ultimately convicted and hanged. Thanks to Hannah Arendt's eyewitness account of the trial, *Eichmann in Jerusalem*, this Nazi has become a lightning rod for intellectual discussions of the moral bankruptcy of our times, when personal responsibility is increasingly tied to one's position in a social hierarchy that expects orders to be executed without question. This distribution of the moral burden renders evil 'banal', in Arendt's famous formulation. But there may be an *upstream* version of the same problem that besets those who give the orders – a *Reverse Eichmann*, as it were.

Special committees of the US Congress and the UK Parliament have conducted hearings into the role of the intelligence services during the Iraq War, given the failure to find the alleged 'weapons of mass destruction' that were the pretext for the war. One pattern revealed by the testimony is that information drawn from aerial photographs and other forms of surveillance was passed among several parties, each of whom provided an interpretation designed to be helpful to the next recipient in the chain of command. The overall result might have been a situation akin to the child's game of 'Chinese whispers' (UK) or 'telephone' (US), in which what began as a blurry image or vague suggestion ended up as a bullet point in US Secretary of State Colin Powell's justification for war, as presented to the UN Security Council in February 2003.

Now suppose that President Bush and Prime Minister Blair have been unwitting victims of this process. To the alert intellectual, the implications go beyond the usual case of spin on overdrive. After all, should they not have questioned more seriously the evidence at their disposal? Based on past experience, they may have had good reason to trust the intelligence services. Nevertheless, given that neither the US nor the UK was already under attack, Bush and Blair had an opportunity to inquire more deeply into the soundness of the inferences drawn from the evidence. But for whatever reason, they did not do so, a point that the parties themselves now seem to admit.

The Eichmann trial established an important moral precedent: trust is no excuse. Eichmann's trust came from a command structure whose evil intent was dissipated once it was rendered as a set of discrete operations. However, in the case of Bush and Blair, evil may have emerged as the unintended consequence of an information flow, no stage of which could be charged with malicious intent. Even so, they still suffered from a failure of negative responsibility. They were sufficiently powerful to have asked questions, and thereby to have acted otherwise. Indeed, unlike Eichmann, who argued that his personal objection to the extermination of Jews would not have altered the Jews' fate, Bush's and Blair's demand for better evidence could have made a difference – at least to all who have subsequently died in Iraq – with minimal damage to their own political standing.

Answers to questions unasked and an evil that emerges from acts unintended: together they conjure an image of

the intellectual in pursuit of shadows that elude the unobservant but, of course, may ultimately turn out to be figments of her own imagination. However, the intellectual's professional paranoia is not without its own brand of romance. In his 1993 Reith Lectures for the BBC, that scourge of 'Orientalists', Edward Said, compared the intellectual to Robin Hood, who legendarily rode around the forests of Nottingham stealing from the rich to give to the poor. This was how Said invited his listeners to think about the task of redressing injustice by giving voice to views – Arab ones, in Said's own case – that would otherwise not be heard properly.

However, Said left out a feature of the medieval legend that updates it in line with Superman, Batman and the other superheroes of mid-20th-century comic strips. Robin Hood was often depicted as a fallen noble, someone who contained within himself a strong element of what he fought against. The human frailty of Jesus in the Gospels is the template for this side of the hero. For nearly all of them, a moment comes when the hero sees in another all that he most despises in himself (and hence distrusts in the other). This moment of repulsion then causes the hero to recognise the ideal he must now come to embody. From that moment, the intellectual *qua* hero internalises both sides of the struggle as eternal vigilance, or paranoia.

Like Batman scouring the night skies of Gotham City for the bat signal requesting his services, the intellectual reads the news as hidden appeals for guidance from a desperate world. The forces of darkness that confront both are typically so subtle in their evil that they elude the normal vehicles of justice. The Anglo-American journalist and self-avowed 'contrarian' Christopher Hitchens embodies the intellectual as the Caped Crusader. For Batman's foes, the Joker and the Riddler, read Mother Teresa and Henry Kissinger – the subjects of two of Hitchens' exposés. Revealing their evil amounts to calling their bluff. This is a risky proposition, since the bluff is maintained through the unwitting complicity of good people and apparently worthy institutions. Thus, to the neutral observer or the moral dupe, it may not be immediately clear who stands for Good and who Evil.

This problem was in ample display in the pages of *The Nation* and the online *Z Magazine* shortly after the destruction of New York's World Trade Center on 11 September 2001. As with the Lisbon earthquake, there was no shortage of judgements about what it all meant and who was ultimately to blame. What perhaps had not been expected was that two leaders of the intellectual left – Hitchens and Noam Chomsky – would portray the situation in such diametrically opposed terms that eventuated in a series of charges and counter-charges, each portraying the other as complicit with evil.

Interestingly, both Chomsky and Hitchens started from the Rousseauian premise that, in an important sense, the US had brought the events of 11 September upon itself by its past treatment of Muslims. However, for Chomsky the terrorism constituted justifiable revenge against America's support for various oppressive regimes in the Islamic world. To prevent future acts of revenge, Chomsky argued, a less self-centred and less aggressive foreign policy would be needed. This appraisal of the situation appalled Hitchens. He argued that the events reflected the West's failure of nerve in stamping out 'Islamofascism', whose 'evil' (Hitchens' word) is evident from the apparent loss of up to 20,000 lives in the suicide-bombing of the Twin Towers. (It is worth recalling that it took nearly a year for the final casualty figure to settle at just under 3,000.) According to Hitchens, the only remedy is greater moral resolve. Thus, he called for a *more* aggressive foreign policy – one reminiscent of the Westernising mission of late-19th-century imperialism – that would finally bring a democratic peace to the Middle East.

With the onset of the Iraq War, versions of these two positions are being played out across the ideological spectrum. For once, the left does not hold a monopoly on self-consuming paranoia.

Stepping back from all these empirical vagaries, philosophers have resorted to logic to defuse paranoia. Their efforts are traceable through the study of *paradox*, that is, the production of two contradictory lines of thought in a single proposition. It would not be unreasonable to consider the philosophical fascination with paradoxes as an academically domesticated way of coping with paranoia, a pathology whose original Greek meaning is 'of two minds'.

Suppose I say, 'I always lie.' Should you believe me? If you believe me, then you're imagining that the status of my lying is something I don't lie about. Bertrand Russell popularised this compartmentalised solution, which privileges the 'second-order' or 'meta-level' voice of the paradox-monger. It is as if, given a split mind, there is an implicit hierarchy by which one part of the mind is presumed to speak authoritatively about the state of the other part.

However, if you don't believe that I always lie, then you're imagining that I lie even about the status of my lying, which implies that I may well tell the truth some of the time, contrary to my claims to be always lying. Much existentialist thought has played with this interpretation of paradox, which denies Russell's neat hierarchy between the two parts of the split mind. For an existentialist like Jean-Paul Sartre, I am always left with a free choice as to which voice in the paradox to believe, for which I alone will then be held accountable.

The heroic intellectual manages her paranoia so as to transcend both Russell's and Sartre's approach to paradox. We might say that Russell's approach holds that Good 'by definition' always triumphs over Evil, whereas Sartre's approach holds that the only difference between Good and Evil rests with whoever ultimately wins our affections. Neither makes for an especially satisfying plot.

Nevertheless, a tincture of both Russell and Sartre can be found in the psyche of the heroic intellectual. She needs Russell for the overall sense of righteous purpose that guides her actions, and she needs Sartre for the compulsion to intervene, since the struggle between Good and Evil always balances on a knife's edge. But additionally, the heroic intellectual must recognise the face of Evil as an aspect of her own soul. In this respect, she must do more than manage her paranoia: she must embrace it. The intellectual becomes a superhero of the mind by having internalised enough Evil to form an immunity to its full-blown version. Without such immunity, the more credulous confront Evil, first, with indifference, then with tolerance, which after a while enables Evil to acquire a taken-for-granted status that soon blends into unwitting submission.

The intellectual, like the superhero, lives in a dualistic universe. Evil is more than the mere absence of Good; it is a well-defined force, even a personality, attractive in many respects and from which much may be learned – but not to the point of giving unconditional loyalty. Indeed, the demand for unconditional loyalty is Evil's calling card, which is why superheroes are on no one's payroll and intellectuals adhere to the (Groucho) Marxist maxim that any party that would claim their allegiance is never worth joining.

This heightened sensitivity to the presence of Evil has often made both intellectuals and superheroes appear mercurial, fickle, and even unreliable, at least from the standpoint of their own secular allies whose fortunes rise and fall with the fates of particular stable social, political and economic structures. Batman's eccentric interventions were as often a source of concern as relief for Gotham City's Police Commissioner. Similarly, France's late great public sociologist Pierre Bourdieu began his career denouncing the state meritocracy in the 1960s as a form of institutionalised racism, only to find himself 30 years later calling for a more resilient state to combat the corruption of social values by market forces. For intellectuals and superheroes, social structures are disposable sites for the ongoing struggle between Good and Evil: what embodies Good one week may embody Evil the next. The heroic intellectual never gives up on the chase.

3. Intellectuals Need a Business Plan

If you want to make money or gain power, you'll regard the intellectual's desire for free inquiry in much the same way: a necessary evil – the more necessary, the more evil

On this much politicians and businesspeople are agreed. The only difference is that, in this case, politicians are more honest. Businesspeople prefer the euphemism 'knowledge management' to 'censorship'. Yet both are hostile to the interests of intellectuals. This harsh verdict has the backing of history. Copyright was introduced in 18th-century Europe as a special case of censorship law: it did on behalf of individuals what had been previously done only on behalf of the state. Originally the only authors who could hold copyright on their words were printers. Even then, 'author' retained the medieval sense of 'authority' that attached more naturally to the impresario editor skilled at selecting the best of what was written than to the writers themselves, who were normally paid a simple wage for their labour without expecting consultation on the final product. Journalism still has much of this character.

Copyright law's original focus on control over the material conditions of idea production encouraged at least temporary monopolies on entire domains of thought. The official reason was to ward off pirate printers who, by not having to pay writers, would flood the market with cheap versions of already published books. However, copyright also had the effect of discouraging legitimate competitors who would have to bear the heavy burden of showing how their 'improvement' on a previous work rose above poorly disguised plagiarism. These strictures encouraged authors to strike out in new directions but not to deal with each other's work in a close and critical fashion.

However, the agitation of writers, buoyed by the Romantic cult of 'genius' of the early 19th century, eventually established writing as a unique form of labour directly covered under copyright. Ownership of a printing press was thus no longer relevant to claims of legal protection for one's words. This marks a turning point in the liberation of ideas from their material containers. Not even the meanest academic publisher worries today that when one author refers a lot to another author's words, she is undercutting the royalties of the second author. On the contrary, academic publishers encourage authors to talk about precisely those authors that everyone else in the field is talking about.

The censorship model of idea regulation may have yielded to the market attractor model, but the overall result is the same: a small fraction of authors – perhaps not the same – are still given most of the attention. All that has changed is that a decision that had been previously taken by one arrogant but responsible party (the censor) is now diffused among many innocent and irresponsible ones (consumers). If you need a definition of the 'dumbing down' of intellectual life, look no further: *marketisation* captures it in a word. Henry Ford, the great automotive pioneer, plays a surprising but important role in this dumbing down of intellectual life. The business philosophy bearing his name, 'Fordism', captures how the academic publishing market has become de-intellectualised.

On the surface, entrepreneurship appears to be exactly the aspect of business that should attract intellectuals. Joseph Schumpeter had figured this out when he described the entrepreneur as the 'creative destroyer' of markets. In other words, the entrepreneur introduces a product whose success with consumers causes her competitors to rethink their market strategy in a funda-mental way: what exactly is the demand we are trying to supply, now that this entrepreneur has managed to capture such a large market share with a radically new product? The entrepreneur causes a change in worldview, the ultimate compliment for an intellectual.

However, Ford spoiled the intellectual's love affair with entrepreneurship when he decided to routinise it. Ford did not want unsold cars accumulating in warehouses once the market was saturated. This would turn Ford into a victim of his own success. Indeed, more generally, economists since Thomas Malthus had traced the cause of depressions to overproduction. Ford's idea was to produce cars to only a tolerable performance standard and always keep inventory stocks low. This would regularise the opportunity to introduce new models into the market. Behind the idea, which later came to be called 'planned obsolescence', is the realisation that a spontaneously occurring behaviour can be manipulated to one's advantage. Thus, Ford thought: drivers eventually need to buy new cars anyway, so why not try to control when they do it? They might then buy cars more often, thereby generating more profits for Ford.

Ford implemented the strategy in his car plants in the 1920s, but it quickly became the house philosophy of the Harvard Business School. By the end of the Second World War, the behavioural psychologist B.F. Skinner would be calling Ford's strategy 'operant conditioning'. Today the two great entrepreneurs of the personal computer, Bill Gates and Steve Jobs, are probably the main beneficiaries of the Ford-Skinner legacy.

However, the strategy of planned obsolescence is also familiar to academic publishers who print a limited run of books of just tolerable quality (in both form and substance), in anticipation that they will sell out just in time for a marginally different book by the same author to hit the market, preferably at the dawn of a new academic year. The result is a proliferation of new editions of textbooks, handbooks and anthologies that compete with each other in presenting largely the same material – plus that 'something extra' which justifies the slight price increase over previous editions. Since intellectual work is already given to self-correction and expansion, publishers have no trouble repackaging those Skinnerian 'operants' as 'incentives' to accelerate the pace of academic labour. Moreover, whatever misgivings academics might have about their complicity with capital are easily removed, once university administrators and their state employers have themselves adopted a capitalist model of cost accounting that rewards greater productivity.

Under the circumstances, the maintenance of product integrity in intellectual life becomes very difficult. If you can plan a product's obsolescence, then presumably you can also anticipate its market replacement. This opens the door to 'speculators' who make short-term bets on what will happen over a longer period. John Maynard Keynes, drawing partly on his own personal experience, understood the mentality of speculators perfectly. They are less concerned with either an investment's intrinsic value or, for that matter, its potential value were it allowed to mature. Rather, they worry about what other speculators *now* think of the investment's prospects. The goal is to benefit from the future before it happens: what is The Next Big Thing? If you want to make a killing, The Next Big Thing need neither be so big nor even much of a thing. What matters is that you are among the first to see through the hype and hence cash in your shares while they still command a high price. We thus enter the virtual realm of *spin*, where more attention is paid to the marketing than the manufacture of products.

Is there anything more to my argument than cynicism propped up by a bad pun on 'speculation'? I am afraid the answer is yes. A generally accepted feature of intellectual speculation that makes it ripe for financial speculation is that high-quality speculations of the first sort – such as the 'scientific revolutions' that reveal something fundamental about reality – are generally unpredictable. This is because they are based on principles that are true regardless of what most people think. Moreover, since people tend to believe things already suited to their interests, the market tends to be biased against the recognition of genuinely new discoveries. On that basis, the savvy investor – say, a state or, more likely, corporate research funder – might seek out interesting long shots that defy the conventional wisdom but, if proved correct, promise a big payoff. These long shots would prove to be the creative destroyers of the intellectual market.

Two fairly obvious features of human inquiry have

tended to put the brakes on speculation. The first is that the perception of novelty is relative to the experience of those currently alive. This is why history – especially of times detached from living memory – has been a perennial source of ideas for shaking up the market. Humanity keeps pursuing variations on the same themes unwittingly. Thus, aspiring intellectual entrepreneurs are advised to look at the latest fad and ask: what have the thundering herd left behind – or forgotten? The answers are eligible to be repackaged as The Next Big Thing.

In the second place, speculation is curbed by what economists call 'opportunity costs': if you want to launch in a new direction, how much of your old investments must you first leave behind or convert? People generally find it hard to believe they have made progress, especially of a revolutionary kind, unless they have had to give up a lot in the process – and, of course, are left standing to tell the tale: what does not kill me makes me stronger.

However, as the natural sciences have become more enveloped in expensive equipment and high training costs, speculators have had to settle for smaller, albeit more frequent, increments of change. Needless to say, the market accommodates to the shift: subtle forms of persuasion diffused over a large space for a long time are replaced by the targeting of particular fields for shorter periods. The speculator no longer worries about being late to pick up on The Next Big Thing. She is more concerned with being late in seeing through the hype of The Last Big Thing.

It is not by accident that the major intellectual breakthroughs of the 20th century associated with relativity theory and quantum mechanics occurred when physics was still a matter of table-top experiments and chalk-and-blackboard calculations. When a scientific revolution could be staged simply by convincing a few élite professors to see the world in radically different terms, at worst a generational change would be needed before the élites were accustomed to the revolutionary views. However, in today's labour-and-capital-intensive 'technoscience', much more is at stake and the sources of resistance much more varied and difficult to overcome with the intellectual's weapon of choice, the force of argument.

A truly revolutionary moment in the intellectual life of the 21st century would be for the scientific establishment to shift to research programmes employing *fewer* people with *less* specialised training working on *smaller* machines at a *lower* cost. Such a shift in thinking would require valuing scientific knowledge more for its *productivity* – the most made from the least – than its sheer *production*, which is the simple outcome of increased resource consumption.

Of course, the humanities and much of the social sciences are still relatively immune to the material limits that increasingly burden speculation in the natural sciences. But from that only follows that these fields are susceptible to *virtualisation*, whereby the course of inquiry simply feeds on itself, spitting out parallel

44

universes that exist alongside the material world we all ordinarily inhabit.

In deference to this tendency, epistemology (the theory of knowing) has yielded to ontology (the theory of being) as the preferred branch of philosophy. Instead of fretting over how to get hold of the one reality to which we are all entitled, many humanists today endeavour to construct alternative realities they can call their own. Differences in epistemic access that had been stigmatised as 'ideology' and diagnosed in terms of 'false conscious-ness' are now dignified with ontic integrity as 'cultures' (note plural), access to which is of concern to members only. Publishers nudge the process along by seeding new journals that promise to 'reconfigure' fields. The jour-nals generate new funding streams by capitalising on the creative capacities of academic language to manufacture new objects of study that are then taken to have 'always already' underwritten the old objects of study. To those not involved, the process looks like a high-minded kind of currency conversion – with publishers acting as bureaux de change.

When more flat-footed intellectuals, often natural scientists, complain about the 'jargon' of humanists, they are referring to this process. The results are likely to appear surreal to those who expect ideas to march lockstep with reality. Instead, ideas appear to flee where reality dares to tread. We live in a time that has witnessed a significant retreat from egalitarianism as an explicit political ideal. Yet this period is also marked by several intellectual attempts to undermine or transcend the distinctions that egalitarianism was designed to address. Rather than seeing to completion the project of redressing discrimination based on class, race and gender, it is now more convenient to deny that these distinctions had mattered very much in the first place. This then becomes the new radicalism of a post-class, post-gender or even post-human world. It demands much of the intellect yet little of the will. Its heralds say, with a straight face, 'Why complain about the growing disparity between the rich and the poor, when the very concern is based on an indefensible privileging of humans over non-humans?'

A good definition of intellectual impotence is that a first-order political failure is reinterpreted as a second-order intellectual virtue. If it sells, it's genius.

Suppose, in spite of what you've read so far, you still want to create a favourable market environment for the reception of your own intellectual entrepreneurship. This involves what the Greek sophists called *ethos* and business gurus today dub 'reputation management'. Here you could do worse than follow the Golden Rule of modern public relations, as laid down by Sigmund Freud's nephew, Edward Bernays. For Bernays the best way to 'engineer consent' is to divert attention from any doubts potential investors might have in your ability to deliver on a set of ideas by stressing the misfortune likely to befall them if the ideas fail to receive adequate investment. Turn the carrot you may never possess into the stick you could then easily produce: *offset uncertainty with risk.*

Take it from Stephen Schneider, the leading public intellectual among US environmental scientists. In justifying the scare-mongering that accompanied his own predictions of 'nuclear winter' in the 1970s and 80s and 'global warming' today, he confessed to *Discover* magazine: 'We need to get some broad-based support to capture the public's imagination. That, of course, entails getting loads of media coverage. So we have to offer up scary scenarios, make simplified, dramatic statements, and make little mention of any doubts we might have. Each of us has to decide what the right balance is between being effective and being honest.'

Call it intellectual blackmail, if you wish, yet Bernays' strategy recalls Pascal's Wager, that 17th-century attempt to revive piety in a world where religious authority was increasingly thrown into doubt. The mathematician Blaise Pascal played off the uncertainty of God's existence against the risk of eternal damnation if God turned out to exist and you had failed to declare your faith. Today Bernays' strategy justifies rather speculative capital-intensive research ventures. Not so long ago we were warned that without a strong commitment to nuclear power, we would run the twin risks of economic dependency and military vulnerability. Now we are threatened with the civilisational meltdown of global warming, if we do not cut down our consumption of fossil fuels and invest in alternative energy sources.

As suits the Keynesian speculator, the empirical force behind these threats is bound to dissolve shortly before they are scheduled to be realised. Thus, the Cold War wound down just before our nuclear captivity was supposed to start, and no doubt more powerful computer models of climate change will eventually temper the nightmare scenarios associated with global warming. Life as we know it depends on our ideas always expiring shortly before they say we should.

In all these cases, what it takes to remain intellectually respectable is exactly what it takes to remain financially solvent: you need to maintain and perhaps even increase commitment – as measured by verbal affirmations and economic investments – until *just before* the bottom falls out of the market for the ideas in question. Jump too early, and you'll appear insensitive to the evidence. But jump too late, and you'll appear to be a mere follower of fashion. In both cases, your own value will decline. Philosophers like to use the word 'irrational' to cover both the 'damned if you do' and the 'damned if you don't' situations. Once again the Greeks had a word for what it takes to appear rational. If the intellectual entrepreneur needs *ethos*, the intellectual investor needs *kairos*, a sense of timing.

In drawing attention to how consent is engineered in the research arena, once again I do not mean to counsel cynicism. Prospects of an unbearable future do not evaporate of their own accord, if nothing is done to prevent their realisation. The hope that one might beat the market for ideas motivates the counter-research efforts that eventually demonstrate that earlier fears have been overstated. The fly in the ointment is *knowledge management*, the hottest research topic in business schools today.

'Knowledge management' sounds like an oxymoron to an intellectual. Things that need to be managed are distrusted in their wild state, such as workers who, without constant supervision, might not focus their energies in the most productive fashion, at least as judged by their employers. However, the production of knowledge *is* supposed to run wild – at least according to the intellectual. Knowledge is something pursued indefinitely, perhaps even profligately, if its pursuit leads in expensive directions involving specialised training, new equipment, etc. Moreover, because the exact import of knowledge is never fully grasped at the time of its creation, those who most heavily invest in knowledge production may turn out *not* to be its main beneficiaries. Nevertheless, the removal of these 'free riding' beneficiaries would be still more costly. This paradoxical situation captures what economists mean when they call knowledge a 'public good'.

The public good conception of knowledge, while still upheld by intellectuals and most academics, harks back to the heyday of the welfare state, when the government raised taxes to subsidise educational and scientific institutions whose specialised work would benefit society as a whole. However, all of this occurred before the law taught us how to convert virtually any piece of knowledge into intellectual property. The trick is to turn it into a piece of *virtual knowledge*, such as a genetic code or a computer program – a second-order machine for producing first-order knowledge.

Knowledge managers may find the public good conception of knowledge passé, but it remains a useful fiction to promote among academics who then underestimate the market value of the research they provide to business. After all, given the unpredictable character of knowledge, why should a firm invest heavily in its own research and development division, when it might easily reap the same benefits at a lower cost by relying on people who act as if knowledge flows as freely as air or water? To those who see at work here the inexorable march of capitalism, the recent state-led initiatives to forge university–industry relations resemble old colonial strategies to foster productivity by exploiting native superstitions. The only difference is that now the natives are our own and they hold doctorates.

When academics had a stronger sense of professional solidarity, the native superstitions could lure potential clients into believing that academic knowledge was superior to that of any non-academic competitor. Typically this involved reference to some unique quality, such as fine theoretical underpinnings, which somehow spoke to the reliability of the knowledge provided but which the client was in no position to inspect for herself. However, the mass proliferation of academic knowledge – or at least credentials – has dissolved this illusion, which economists now disparage as 'rent seeking' behaviour. Instead academics are forced to chase, not dictate, the market. Perhaps then they would be better off charging industry rates for their services. At the very least, it would test the firm on its exact commitment to knowledge production. This is likely to prove minimal. Rather than pay exorbitant sums for uncertain results, the firm's knowledge manager would revert to the age-old business strategy of 'Outsource or own'. In other words, in a knowledge-based domain where the firm is competitive, if exploitable academics are unavailable, then convert an otherwise fluid line of inquiry into a piece of intellectual property on which you can collect rent from those who wish to develop it further. At this point, the true intellectual turns into an anarchist of the second order.

4. Intellectuals Want the Whole Truth

If lying is telling a falsehood with the intent to deceive, then there are two ways of not lying. The first involves telling the truth with the intent to deceive, the second telling a falsehood with the intent not to deceive. Those who claim to tell the truth without deception err on the side of the former, whereas intellectuals, who do not harbour such illusions, err on the side of the latter.

Truth is the ultimate conversation stopper. At the very least, when someone claims access to the truth, the stakes of continuing the conversation are raised. However, the history of Western thought provides two rather different ways of thinking about truth. The first is focused on *only the truth*, and the second *the whole truth*. Philosophers know them as the 'correspondence' and 'coherence' theories of truth. Each answers a different question. The former asks: does this claim correspond to reality (or does it miss the mark)? The latter asks: is reality all that is claimed (or has something crucial been left out)?

Courtroom trials purport to produce 'the whole truth and nothing but the truth'. Unfortunately, as intellectuals know all too well, the two tendencies trade off against each other. A focus on 'nothing but the truth' is rather conservative: one errs on the side of excluding uncertainties out of fear they might mask falsehoods. In contrast, a focus on 'the whole truth' is more liberal: one errs on the side of including uncertainties in the hope they might reveal truths. Even the law itself implicitly recognises the dilemma in its endless wranglings over its 'letter' versus its 'spirit'.

What hangs in the balance? Let's start with a homely example. Suppose I say, 'It is raining' and it happens to be raining. To someone seeking only the truth, I have indeed spoken the truth. But what if the rain stops in a few minutes and you end up carrying your umbrella unnecessarily for the rest of the day? You might conclude that my original assertion was misleading, and it would have been better to say, 'It is not raining'. That is how the situation looks to someone concerned with the whole truth.

Journalists routinely face this problem of interpretation in their quest for truth. A good case in point came up in the UK's Hutton Inquiry, which looked into whether the government had 'sexed up' the military threat posed by Iraq in the run-up to the 2003 war. Two BBC reporters, Susan Watts and Andrew Gilligan, spoke to the same principals but drew radically different conclusions. Watts found no evidence that the government tried to spin military intelligence in favour of war, whereas Gilligan did. The Inquiry sided with Watts, operating within a narrow 'only the truth' remit. However, it is now clear that even if the government did not force the hand of the intelligence agencies, it was set to interpret whatever they provided as a case for going to war.

The import of the two opposing attitudes to truth is arresting. Is truth something built like a wall, one brick at a time? Or is it more like an image that gradually comes into focus as a whole? Lord Hutton agreed with Watts that at no point did the government force the intelligence agencies to report something they did not believe to be the case. In that formal sense, the integrity of the agencies was not politically compromised. But perhaps that is not the standard that should have been applied. Rather, one might have looked for emergent patterns in the government's behaviour over a longer period, especially in relation to other patterns that might have emerged instead. That would have vindicated Gilligan.

Putting a brave face on the Hutton Inquiry, we might see here an important reason for the separation of powers in a democracy between the judiciary and the legislature. An appointed judiciary may be especially good at determining only the truth, whereas an elected legislature may be needed to get at the whole truth. Journalists then occupy the unenviable position of unelected legislators – unenviable, that is, except to intellectuals.

Experts and censors focus on 'only the truth' to pre-empt disagreement and reinforce their own voices, while intellectuals fixate on 'the whole truth' to inject unheard voices potentially capable of resolving disagreement and overturning orthodoxies. However, the intellectual need not herself have access to these unheard voices. The bare possibility – unaddressed and hence unrefuted – that such other voices exist is sufficient to motivate her inquiries. In this respect, the intellectual unashamedly appeals to the *imagination* as a source of evidence. This move is itself an endless source of friction between intellectuals and most academics, especially philosophers and scientists, who scrupulously trade in only the truth. The friction is in open view whenever academics refer to intellectuals as 'literary', a derogatory term for someone who indiscriminately moves between what academics call 'fact' and 'fiction' – or how 'only the truth' and 'the whole truth', respectively, appear to those with an interest in keeping them studiously apart.

Here a little sociology goes a long way. The history of so-called literary intellectuals is strewn with the careers of disappointed academics, frustrated civil servants, bored bank clerks and sidelined clerics. They are people who have involuntarily landed in the peripheries of knowledge production. Adjusting to their fate, they appoint themselves as a government-in-exile or loyal opposition who retrieve and rework ideas forgotten or demoted by the mainstream. Historically the main medium for transmitting these marginalised ideas has not been writing but sheer living. For the most part, women, children, migrants, slaves and labourers have embodied their ideas in themselves, the things they have produced and the shape they have given to their environments.

The predominance of writing as the *lingua franca* of authoritative ideas testifies to the subtle influence of academics who down through the ages have been hired to provide the dominant political and economic ideas with a stability and portability those ideas would otherwise lack. However, since marginalised ideas do not enjoy the benefits accrued to academic canonisation, their status as evidence is always suspect. After all, how does one establish 'only the truth' about the ideas conveyed in a lowly gesture or artefact? Not surprisingly, then, the great unwritten record of intellectual life – the proper domain of the imagination – is often conceived as the seat of a 'collective unconscious' just waiting to be tapped and given its due documentation. Perhaps the exemplary work in this genre, Howard Zinn's *A People's History of the United States*, was written by a professional academic who turned to a commercial publisher to transcend the usual academic strictures.

The signature moment in the history of intellectuals – Emile Zola's 'J'Accuse!' – was a blatant exercise of the imagination that could never have come from a proper academic. Zola, a celebrated champion of naturalism in the French novel, published an open letter to the editor of *L'Aurore* that appeared on the front page of the 13 January 1898 edition. He accused the French War Office of framing Captain Alfred Dreyfus, a Jew who had been sent to the penal colony Devil's Island four years earlier for allegedly having sold state secrets to the Germans. Much, though by no means all, of the French public had been willing to believe the charges against Dreyfus, who was the perfect scapegoat for nostalgic Bonapartists and Bourbons unable to face the French Republic's declining political fortunes on the world stage.

However, Zola himself was not an investigative journalist in possession of some decisive memorandum that proved prevarication. He simply read between the lines of what had already been published about the case and articulated what he thought remained to be said. Indeed, Zola was prosecuted and found guilty of libel because he lacked evidence of a cover-up. His vindication came only after the confession of one of the perpetrators.

It would be mistaken to conclude that literary figures are unique in their appeal to the imagination to get at the whole truth – even if at the expense of only the truth. No less than Galileo, that 17th-century icon of scientific

heroism, overplayed his hand by fabricating experimental results and embellishing observational accounts
– and then claiming these contradicted the centuries-old
authority of Aristotle, Ptolemy and Scripture. Even
Galileo's most sympathetic critics found his appeal to the
telescope as a scientific instrument rather puzzling. He
lacked a principled explanation – a theory of optics – for
how this Dutch toy, essentially a spyglass, enabled him to
see lunar craters and sunspots. Moreover, the lenses that
Galileo improvised for his own telescope were so full of
distortion that observers not already convinced of his
interpretation could make little sense of what they saw
through them. When pressed by his Catholic Inquisitors
to justify his hyperbole, Galileo sometimes retreated to
a more modest position. He argued that his vivid
presentation of counter-intuitive hypotheses offered an
opportunity for his opponents to clarify the grounds on
which the orthodoxy should be maintained.

No historian today believes that Galileo actually held
such an objective view of his own work, but his response
remains relevant to scientists who fancy themselves as
intellectuals. The public image of scientists as detached
and cautious experts is not inherent to the conduct of
science but merely to its public image as a 'value-neutral'
enterprise above and beyond political wrangling. As
Karl Popper saw perhaps most clearly, scientists *qua*
scientists advance the course of inquiry precisely by
overstating their knowledge claims, or going beyond

the data. However, at the same time, Popper envisaged that these bold inquirers would be subject to stiff cross-examination, possibly resulting in a falsification of their claims. Contrary to Popper's celebrated antagonist Thomas Kuhn, science is a distinctly *social* enterprise not because all scientists genuflect to the dominant paradigm but because they are forever in a state of managed conflict with each other.

The failure of Popper's vision to be realised speaks more to the organisation of contemporary scientific inquiry than to the character of individual scientists. There are few incentives and many disincentives for scientists to challenge ideas that already enjoy prima facie support or, as in Galileo's own case, to put forward ideas that go against the grain and perhaps cannot yet be fully substantiated. It is a commonplace for philosophers and sociologists of science to argue that scientists must be as scrupulous as possible in their research because their colleagues are rarely in a position to check their work and much often hangs in the balance. Thus, something called 'trust' among mutually recognised scientists in a given field – the 'peers' of the 'peer review process' – continually greases the wheels of inquiry.

This argument should give the intellectual pause. It implies that scientists live a schizoid existence. They are supposed to be professional inquisitors – but only of nature, not each other. Two kinds of questions then come to mind. First, why do scientists have such great problems validating each other's work? One obvious possibility is sheer lack of competence. However, if that were the true answer, science would be reduced to an elaborate confidence game. A more acceptable answer is that endeavouring to validate another scientist's research would be too time-consuming. Presupposed here is the idea that the research frontier advances at a fast pace that cannot be easily arrested. But why is that? The answer probably has little to do with the nature of scientific research and much with the political and economic interests that stand to gain by the acceleration of inquiry.

The second kind of question is bound to be more controversial: does it really matter if scientists fail to catch their own errors? Sometimes invoking Galileo, scientists like to believe that science is so organised that all error is eventually caught. However, it is difficult to establish the empirical basis for this claim, since, by definition, we know only of the cases where errors have been committed and corrected. We don't know about the undetected errors, though we do know that when scientists have an incentive to find error – perhaps because the research topic is highly competitive, lucrative or consequential – they tend to find more error. What then follows? Only wishful thinking would suggest that science is somehow 'self-correcting', such that all errors eventually cancel each other out and we are left with the unvarnished truth. It is more likely that reality can tolerate a great many of the truths and errors we might come to believe and, just as intellectuals would expect, it is for the scientific community – and the supporting society – to decide the ones for which it wishes to be held responsible. Only then is the truth made whole.

THE INTELLECTUAL AND THE
PHILOSOPHER: A DIALOGUE

How, exactly, shall the truth set you free?

PHILOSOPHER: I must say that while I respect your attempts to enlighten people on various aspects of their world, I really think you cut corners in trying to make your points. In that respect, you compromise the values of truth and reason you claim to uphold.

INTELLECTUAL: How so?

P: I don't pretend to have catalogued all your philosophical misdemeanours, but many of them can be captured in one point: *you reduce much of the real complexity of what you talk about.* You collapse a lot of distinctions that philosophers and other academics have been careful to draw. This may help focus your moral fervour, but it also contributes to a polarised world-view – a 'them versus us' mentality – that ultimately generates more heat than light. Presumably, you want to be able to fight the good fight without either attacking straw men or tilting at windmills.

I: Can you give me an example of when I've crossed your imaginary line?

P: I read somewhere that you claimed Americans are so

narcissistic that they care about violence overseas only when American people and interests are threatened. What is your evidence for such an inflammatory statement?

I: Of course, I don't know whether all – or even most – Americans think this way.

P: So then why do you perpetuate this unflattering stereotype in public forums?

I: Well, first of all, it's not clear whether the stereotype is true or false. I realise that philosophers believe that something should be asserted only when you know – or at least think you know – it's true. But is this modest stance really based on a sound theory of knowledge or simply fear of giving offence to the powerful? In a world we already know to be unjust, it is unreasonable to place the burden of proof on someone trying to speak truth to power. If Americans are not as narcissistic as I allege, then they should have no trouble proving me wrong – say, by reminding me of relevant policy initiatives.

P: But don't you think Americans have better things to do than help you conduct your education in public? You don't seem to appreciate that it's *your* responsibility to be informed about the things you pass judgement on.

I: You clearly fail to see what it is to be an intellectual. If everyone had to be as informed as you suggest before entering the public sphere, then very soon it would consist only of experts talking to each other. Intellectuals insist on having their education conducted in public because we write and speak on behalf of the ordinary citizen. Ordinary people are fallible in many respects –

bad memory, bad reasoning, bad judgement, and so on. In this respect, the intellectual hopes to make instructive mistakes that serve to enhance society's 'collective intelligence', an entity whose consistency is much closer to that of common sense than to a body of academic knowledge.

P: Once we cut through the self-serving rhetoric, what you've just said sounds like a very pessimistic view about our ability to learn collectively from experience.

I: Of course, I don't deny that we learn from experience. But at the same time, experience doesn't sit in our memories in suspended animation. It too changes over time. It is forgotten and distorted. You shouldn't suppose that every event is recorded by some great historian in the sky and we all have equal access to what the historian has written. In any case, you need to look at the bright side of all this fallibility. Suppose history repeats itself because we never quite learn its lessons the first time. That means we get a second chance to either reaffirm what has been taken for granted or change course altogether. After all, my American readers may find themselves incapable of proving that they are *not* narcissistic. That fact alone might cause Americans to think twice the next time they elect a president.

P: I see! You make a virtue out of a liability. By the logic of your argument, it follows that to forget is to be free. I thought intellectuals stuck to the old Enlightenment motto, 'The truth shall set you free'.

I: There is no inconsistency here. In a nutshell, the

intellectual uses Nietzsche to undo the damage of Hegel. Hegel held that the powerful are the principal agents of history, and even though they couldn't exactly bend history to their will, Hegel's point was that they nevertheless had the ability to convert their perspective into the orthodoxy, at least in the short term. If Hegel had his way, we would be forever burdened with history as a succession of orthodoxies. Our options would become increasingly limited as we were forced to manoeuvre within the constraints laid down by our mighty ancestors. Academics, especially scientists in the grip of what Thomas Kuhn called a 'paradigm', overestimate this self-imposed prison of thought. (And you say *I* make a virtue out of a liability!) In contrast, Friedrich Nietzsche started life as a precocious student of the Greek classics, but he eventually dropped out of academia because he refused to believe that we have been bequeathed a perfect record of the past, on the basis of which we are obliged to build. Rather, he believed that the past is always under construction – which effectively means under contestation and ripe for reinvention. The prospect of an open past is both scary and liberating. Nietzsche himself took permanent sick leave after his first book, *The Birth of Tragedy*, received a bad review.

P: Even lacking Nietzsche's tender sensibilities, I can see the idea of an open past as scary – but liberating?

I: Precisely in the sense of 'The truth shall set you free'. After all, whatever else may be true, this certainly is: our collective memory is sufficiently faulty, by both design and default, that any inclination we might have to believe that something *must* be either true or false – that it could not be otherwise – should be treated as a failure of the imagination rather than a recognition of ultimate reality. This is why the only reliable means to the truth is *criticism*. Of course, criticism does not always hit its target, but there is no weapon quite like it in the intellectual's arsenal.

P: Now you sound wildly idealistic – as if we could simply think ourselves out of the certitudes of the laws of physics! I assure you that no matter how cleverly you deconstruct the history of science to show any number of directions it could have gone, the fact remains that if you walk out of this window, you will fall down and make a big splat! And even if I grant you that physics has been the handmaiden of power and capital, rather than a vehicle of liberation, those basic facts will not go away.

I: Here, I fear, you are the one guilty of collapsing a key distinction upheld by the scholastics, academics whom I would normally oppose for their excessively curatorial attitude towards knowledge: a distinction between *the fact* and *the reasoned fact*. We might say there are many ways to fall out of a window, and the one we choose matters. Yes, in all cases, I fall down. Nevertheless, what happens next depends on whether we think of this fact as an insurmountable barrier or a soluble problem. Put crudely but not inaccurately, *we can think away facts by turning them into problems*. Moreover, this is not some wild-eyed idealism. It's how best to think about the historic relationship between engineering and Newtonian physics or, for that matter, biomedical science and Darwinian natural selection. The spirit of your remarks notwithstanding, we did not respond to the discovery of the law of falling bodies by avoiding heights – and we certainly didn't respond to the survival of the fittest by accepting death more willingly. (Richard Dawkins and Peter Singer may be honourable exceptions here.) In both cases, the supposedly brute facts captured in these 'laws of nature' became challenges to our ingenuity.

P: But all this 'ingenuity' was the work of scientists, not wordsmiths like you …

I: … or you philosophers, for that matter. My point is that these scientists have exactly the same attitude towards so-called 'brute facts' as intellectuals: we are both suspicious of their finality. The brute quality of these facts is symptomatic of an obstacle in the progress of our thought. We may have forgotten something or someone may be trying to block our passage.

P: It sounds to me like you're trying to make a virtue out of impatience. I suppose this is understandable, considering your tight deadlines and limited column inches …

I: … sorry, I must stop you right there. I think you've got matters backwards. Intellectuals are not philosophers operating under unfortunate time and space constraints. Rather, philosophers are intellectuals operating under different versions of the same constraints, except that philosophers do not see them as constraints. Instead you wear them as badges of professionalism.

P: What could you possibly mean – other than to insult me?

I: Well, philosophers are not completely absent from public intellectual life. The two main species of philosopher these days – the continental and the analytic – have their characteristic ways of simplifying the complexities of reality. The continental philosophers take their marching orders from France and Germany, while the analytic philosophers hold firm on the superiority of Anglophone thought. Nevertheless, from the standpoint of public intellectual life, what matters is that both types are creatures of the classroom who are loosened up a bit to fit a world of sound bites and short attention spans.

P: I still find it hard to recognise what you're talking about.

One-stop shopping for the mind: the case of continental philosophy

I: Take continental philosophers first. The better ones are given a bit more slack in public intellectual life, but that's because their words are valued more for the idiosyncratic mood set by their prose than the specificity of their message. Consequently, newspaper and magazine editors often treat them with kid gloves – as they would a novelist whose work they're excerpting for publication. Of course, the philosophers themselves believe that their words and ideas are inextricably tied together.

P: It sounds to me like these philosophers have some clout with the editors. Do I detect a hint of envy in your remarks?

I: I may be jealous but I am not envious. After all, if a certain idea must be expressed in a certain way, it could be for two radically different reasons: either the ideas are so unique that any other form of words would miss the point, or the ideas have no meaning beyond the words on the page. The main problem with continental philosophers is that they don't try to distinguish between these two possibilities.

P: And what do you think they do instead?

I: Continental philosophers like to crawl under the skin of some 'master thinker' of French or German origin, recycling his thought by speaking his words in new contexts. (The better philosophers of this type can crawl under the skins of two or three such thinkers.) The master thinkers have something to say about everything. What is most interesting is not any particular thing they say but how it all hangs together – usually with the help of some neologisms that mask contentious assumptions. These philosophers are attractive because they provide *one-stop shopping for the mind.* Once you've learned to think like, say, Michel Foucault or Jürgen Habermas, you never need to think for yourself again. Of course, there is wide scope of application and even emendation of the master thinker's thoughts, but the fundamentals are beyond question. For people who dread continually having to make decisions about what to think, the prospect of one-stop shopping is quite a relief.

P: Your sarcasm is not appreciated. Whatever else one might say about Foucault and Habermas, they certainly tried to arrive at a comprehensive understanding of matters that would otherwise remain confined to disparate fields. No one before Foucault had explored with equal measures of historical and philosophical insight the full range of anxieties surrounding the human body that have implicitly motivated the career of reason in the West. As for Habermas, no one else in our era has drawn together the full range of rationalist traditions – both continental and analytic – in persistent defence of liberal values and humanity more generally. Moreover, each in his own way manifested a concern for the underdog and the dispossessed that so precisely defines intellectuals. So why slur Foucault and Habermas?

I: I did not make myself clear. I have no problem with Foucault or Habermas, only with their epigones, clones and affiliated drones. Here I confess a special animus towards continental philosophy when conducted in the English-speaking world – that is, by the intellectual colonials. It's the classic case of the disciples doing the master a disservice by miming his words but missing his deeds. They create a church where a mission is really required. If the disciples tried to come up with their own original syntheses, or outdo the master in following through the implications of his ideas – or better still,

reinvent the master's role in their own time and place –
then they would command my respect.

P: I think you demand too much intellectual heroism
from philosophers …

I: Well, it hasn't always been so much. What I have just
proposed describes the relationship between Immanuel
Kant and the German idealists Fichte, Schelling, Schlei-
ermacher, Schlegel, Hegel, Schopenhauer, Feuerbach
and a host of lesser figures who flourished in the half-
century following the publication of *The Critique of Pure
Reason* in 1781. This was the first modern generation
of philosophers who earned a living as professional
academics, indeed, as Prussian civil servants. And they
were all still intellectuals.

P: I'm surprised you can talk this way about the
idealists. Their writings are impenetrable and arguably
the source of the worst verbal mannerisms in continental
philosophy today. How can they exemplify the sort of
public intellectual you extol?

I: I don't dispute the idealists' mannerist legacy. But
once again this is because their followers imitate the
word and ignore the deed. The idealists' overly com-
pressed mode of expression merely shows that their
writing was meant to complement, not replace, speech.
As masters of rhetoric, they treated the combination of
speech and writing as a multimedia activity – albeit
rather low-tech by today's standards! Theirs was the
compression of *aides-memoires*, of lecture notes. At the
moment of delivery, the notes were enlivened with

anecdotes, examples and puns that immediately concretised the abstractions, triggering illumination in the target audience. Of course, these spoken elements would differ according to occasion – and why not? It only showed that the idealists were willing and able to appeal directly to the audience by recasting their ideas for maximum impact. Not surprisingly, they are the philosophers who have taken most seriously our capacity for *wit*.

P: This sounds like an unduly charitable gloss on what in practice was obscurantist mystification.

I: Oh yeah? And *whose* practice are we talking about here? Consider a recent master of this kind of philosophising, Theodor Adorno, the doyen of the Frankfurt School from which Habermas descends. He was a notorious defender of difficult writing, and his writing is notoriously difficult. However, Adorno's last set of lectures in philosophy and sociology, delivered at the University of Frankfurt in the 1968–9 academic year, were taped and transcribed. Their lucidity and brilliance make them the best possible introduction to his thought. But it is hard to imagine that Adorno could have produced the lectures as a pure piece of writing. That they exist in this form at all is not unrelated to the fact that Adorno has now been dead for several decades. In any case, how do you suppose that someone like Martin Heidegger managed to have such a profound impact on his students? Do you think he was simply reading them drafts of his impenetrable prose?

P: Well, if what you say is true, then how did the rot set in? On your telling, most continental philosophy these days is intellectually corrupt.

I: True, and the source of the corruption serves as a cautionary tale about the perils of institutionalising the work of the intellectual. In 1973, the Yale literary critic Harold Bloom published a short work that established his own reputation as a public intellectual, *The Anxiety of Influence*. Bloom argued that writers establish their originality by engaging in a para-Oedipal act of killing the literary father, the person who most influenced their writing and hence with whom they strive *not* to be associated. There is much truth to this thesis – and the truth it speaks is not necessarily bad. However, if the father casts a very large shadow, then the children are not so ashamed to compete for his legacy openly by repeatedly invoking his name and citing his words.

P: For example?

I: Consider the endless squabbles among the intellectual progeny of Marx and Freud. When they occurred outside the academy, the squabbles were tied to some 'real world' input that bore on the efficacy of particular political or therapeutic strategies associated with The Great Man's name. However, starting in the 1960s, faced with mounting empirical failures, both the Marxists and the Freudians retreated to the Ivory Tower. Nowadays they have become 'deep readers' of each other's texts, convinced that some proper weighting of the canonical corpus will reveal the mysteries of the universe.

P: And one would never have to think for oneself again?

I: At the very least, one would never again have to *think in one's own name* – that is, take personal responsibility for one's ideas. One would simply think in the name of the father: as I said before, one-stop shopping for the mind. One person who is brutally honest on this point is Slavoj Žižek, a polyglot Slovenian intellectual known for his ability to convert popular culture into footnotes to Marx and Freud in real time. He once confessed in an old gossip sheet for American intellectuals, *Lingua Franca*, that his career goal is to be Jacques Lacan's Thomas Aquinas.

P: What could that possibly mean?

I: Lacan brought psychoanalysis to France in the 1930s. He interpreted the unconscious as a language that simultaneously permits and prohibits the expression of desire. As Lacan began to be translated into English in the 1960s, he rode the wave of Noam Chomsky's psychologically credible and scientifically respectable 'generative grammar', the supposed substructure of rational thought. Once again, thanks to diligent epigones, clones and drones, Lacan and Chomsky were soon 'intertextualised' as part of a common 'structuralist' movement in the human sciences – without the consent of either master! As for Aquinas, well, he lived seven centuries earlier and is now the official philosopher of the Roman Catholic Church. He earned this status on the basis of several systematic works designed to defend the faith from all manner of infidels. He had an answer for everything, typically splitting differences whenever possible, while remaining on the right side of orthodoxy. While Aquinas' defences seemed contrived to many of his contemporaries, nevertheless over the centuries, as the Church faced greater challenges to its authority, the virtues of his approach came to be more widely appreciated – and ultimately rewarded with canonisation.

P: OK. So Žižek wants to be remembered as the Great Defender of the Freudian Faith. But what's the point of that these days, given the general disrepute of psychoanalysis as a therapeutic practice?

I: Good question! Speaking charitably, I suppose Žižek intends his fantasy *Summa Lacanica* as a blueprint for a government in exile. In other words, he imagines that today's negative estimation of Freudianism is a temporary aberration that with enough perseverance will be reversed in the future. There is certainly precedent for such a project in the annals of intellectuals. Jean-Paul Sartre spoke of his involvement in the French Resistance against the Nazis in such terms, and 'the return of the repressed' remains a rallying cry for post-colonial intellectuals the world over.

P: And how exactly does Žižek envisage this 'Second Coming' taking place?

I: Well, he doesn't – or at least he is not counting on it. Unlike Sartre and the post-colonialists, who explain their opposition in terms that enable them to go forward, Žižek can't explain the eclipse of Freud except by giving Freudian explanations for the 'resistance' displayed by anti-Freudians. Failed therapies and dubious politics travelling under Freud's own name don't figure in his thinking at all.

P: Well, then, what does?

I: Žižek relies on the shared faith of his primary audience, mainly academics and their hangers-on, all more or less adept in the Freudian corpus. For these people, Žižek matters less for his revolutionary vision than for his versatility in applying Freud to say darkly sparkling things about current events, including the latest films! After a while this stuff, which regularly graces the pages of *The London Review of Books*, starts to look like a boring party trick. So the 'government in exile' interpretation of Žižek's activities may be a bit of a stretch, on second thought …

P: Your criticism of Žižek makes me suspect that you're really making a general complaint about the way knowledge is produced and transmitted in universities. Žižek has merely made a virtue out of something you regard as a liability. Your hostility to the scholastic tendencies of academics betrays, I dare say, the intellectual's own brand of anti-intellectualism.

I: Historically you've got a point. Erasmus, Galileo and Voltaire immediately spring to mind as exemplars of the peculiar brand of 'anti-intellectualism' you detect in my words. But I have even more reason than they did for anti-scholasticism. At least their scholastics did not pretend to be progressive thinkers on the cusp of history. Scholastics were quite self-consciously upholders of an establishment that Erasmus, Galileo and Voltaire set out to undermine. However, today's continental philosophers are routinely treated as 'radicals' in that politically vague sense with which only English-speakers are entirely comfortable. Often all that seems to matter is that these philosophers are saying something outré.

P: But what about all that 'deep reading' you earlier disparaged – doesn't that suggest that some kind of intellectual discipline is involved? Perhaps there is more to continental philosophy than merely its shock value.

I: I do not wish to deny that there is a method to this madness, but it is a mad method. Continental philosophers are often difficult to understand simply because they insist on expressing themselves in very restricted terms – typically those set by one or a few 'master thinkers'. Here is a way to think about this problem, which I hope isn't too much of a parody. Suppose I were trained as an engineer, but I read a little continental philosophy along the way and, as a result, became a 'deep reader' of the physics on which my engineering relies. I might decry the 'hegemonic' influence of Newtonian mechanics for 'repressing' the voices of the earlier theories Newton displaced. So far there is no problem, at least as far as I am concerned.

P: Well, I already have a problem with how you've politicised the history of science …

I: Yes, and that's why you're a philosopher and I'm an intellectual. But we'll get back to that point later. For now, I want to say that the problem really starts once this 'deep' engineer decides that the solution lies *not* in figuring out how to incorporate the lost insights of the past in the terms of modern science, but rather in reconstructing modern science in terms of the lost insights. In other words, imagine what it would be like to reconstruct Newtonian mechanics, which still captures the physical basis of engineering, by operating entirely within theories Newton had rendered obsolete, such as Aristotle's physics and Ptolemy's astronomy – both of which had the sun and all the planets surrounding the earth. I suppose it could be done, given enough patience and ingenuity. After all, the Vatican continues to conduct its business in Latin by devoting an entire bureau to coining neologisms for a world that Cicero and Pliny could never have envisaged. But what is the point?

P: I grant you that this is not the royal road to truth. Still, you have to admit there is a certain principled intellectual virtuosity to being able to say things in languages not designed to say them.

I: Principled? It is more a way to avoid admitting error and thereby having to learn new things. The practice displays a profound lack of openness towards the world, a refusal to be bold in the face of vulnerability. Again think Vatican City.

P: But surely you grant that no language is perfect. Certain things can't be expressed effectively – for whatever reason – unless one engages in difficult modes of speech and writing.

I: Of course, I grant this – but only as a brute fact, not a badge of honour! All difficulty is not created equal.

Understanding the source of difficulty is crucial. One legitimate source of difficult expression is the kind of repression you just dismissed as 'politicised'. It is always a mistake to think that language binds us together like the proverbial social contract in which each consents to be governed by all. The general recognition of acceptable and unacceptable modes of speech is the subtlest form of social power, mainly because it is self-administered. We stop ourselves from saying things because we don't want to lose face. Those with less effective power have more to lose with the more they say. This is perhaps Foucault's profoundest lesson, one that places him in the upper echelons of intellectuals.

P: So then what would be an example of an *illegitimate* source of difficult expression?

I: This happens any time a continental philosopher tries to leverage linguistic poverty into intellectual richness. Put another way, difficulty is illegitimately manufactured whenever an absence of empirical breadth is mistaken for the presence of conceptual depth. Say you restrict yourself to speaking in the name of Marx and Freud, and then address things that cast doubt on what they said, such as the absence of a proletarian revolution or the presence of post-Oedipal identity formation. Not surprisingly, you end up saying some rather complicated and paradoxical things. But you have succeeded only in engaging in some roundabout speech that could have been avoided, had you availed yourself of a less sectarian vocabulary. But the continental philosophical game is mostly about deep reading and roundabout speech. By the time you have gone to the trouble of learning the relevant codes, you will have become an 'insider', capable of wielding a sort of esoteric power by virtue of that fact alone. This is a trick that the US continental philosopher and queer theorist Judith Butler learned from Plato.

P: What! How so? All I know about Butler is that a few years ago she won the 'Bad Writing' contest awarded each year by the editors of the journal *Philosophy and Literature*. So she must not have been that successful.

I: *Au contraire.* In fact, the editors played right into Butler's hands, though neither she nor they appreciated it at the time. An accusation of 'Bad Writing' boils down to the charge that the author doesn't know what she's talking about. In fact, of course, it implies only that the accuser doesn't know what the author is talking about – and hopes that others share this problem.

P: But why worry about Butler's literary malfeasance in the first place?

I: Exactly the point! That she is accused at all is already a major concession to her power. (This is why intellectuals like to make accusations: we want to force the accused to reveal the power they're trying to hide.) So all that Butler had to do after her opponents' opening blunder was to use the least force possible in displaying her power, preferably by conveying magnanimity. In short: don't insult the accuser. Butler managed this in no less than *The New York Times*. She portrayed difficult writing as a kind of self-sacrifice that few have either the will or the opportunity to perform. The reader was left believing that Butler and her fellow travellers write as great explorers sailing to uncharted regions under the flag of Humanity.

P: Once again, I detect a note of sarcasm in your analysis. So what's the point?

I: The point is that accusations of 'Bad Writing' merely reinforce the sort of difficult writing championed by Butler and others influenced by continental philosophy. The real problem isn't that Butler doesn't know what she's talking about. *The problem is that what she's talking about isn't best served by what she knows.* She has clearly raised some important issues relating to gender identity, especially once the biological basis of sexuality is called into question. These issues are bound to loom large in law and politics in the coming years, especially as developments in medical research and biotechnology allow for various cross-gendered possibilities that go well beyond cross-dressing: suppose people could easily undergo a sex change or be equipped to perform a role traditionally restricted to one sex – such as carrying a pregnancy to term? However, you can't get very far addressing these questions if you're armed with little more than a pastiche of recent French post-structuralist thought. What you get instead is rather like what anthropologists used to call a 'cargo cult', whereby the Third World (or in this case, American) natives come to worship the packaging that carries the First World (French) relief aid rather than its actual contents.

P: If what you say is true, then why don't continental philosophers try to change this situation, so that they don't end up in Butler's cul-de-sac?

I: The short answer is that these philosophers welcome their predicament, and academia gives them no reason to do otherwise. After all, Butler is one of the most highly cited academics today, perhaps the most highly cited woman. Continental philosophers suffer from what social psychologists call *adaptive preference formation*. This is popularly known as 'sour grapes' – and its converse is 'sweet lemons'. We have lots of clever ways of persuading ourselves that a simple error is really a profound truth, that an apparent misfortune is a blessing in disguise. Now, as an intellectual, I am especially sensitive to this phenomenon because very often things are not at all as they seem, especially when seen from a wider perspective. However, this broadened horizon can easily turn into an adaptive preference if it merely enables people to cope with a reality they have come to believe cannot be changed. A very vivid documentation of adaptive preference formation is the series of films that Michael Apted has done under the rubric 'Seven Up', which consists simply of interviews with people from different classes in British society at seven-year intervals, starting when they are aged seven. (In the latest instalment, the interviewees were 42.) The interviews generally encourage the people to think about their lives in narrative terms: where did they come from, where have they been and where are they going? It is especially eerie to watch how all the interviewees adapt their narratives to circumstances beyond their control.

P: OK, but how does all this apply to continental philosophers?

I: Well, I have been struck by the self-serving perspective shared by many of these philosophers, Butler included. The perspective unfolds in four stages. First, the philosopher shifts the focus from reality as such to its conceptualisation. Thus, we might hear nothing about society but lots about how the word 'society' is used – or, better still, *not* used. This is meant to give the impression that the philosopher is tracking the power that comes from having access to the means of expression ...

P: But given your reverence for Foucault, you could not possibly object to that as an opening move.

I: The first stage is fine. The problems start afterwards. In the second stage, the philosopher claims that by fixating on word use, she can transcend how reality is – indeed, get at the full range of how reality can be (or, more precisely, how it can be said to be). Yet, third, the effects of these words are also claimed to be always indeterminate. So the philosopher appears capable of making sense of more while exerting control over less. The final twist is that these effects are presented as implying not philosophy's impotence or irrelevance but reality's capacity to generate novelty in a way that only the philosopher can appreciate.

P: But how is all this traceable to adaptive preferences?

I: I suspect that these philosophers missed the irony

hidden in Keynes' quip that every politician is in the thrall of some long-dead economist. The operative word is 'dead'. The continental philosophical imagination appears so 'powerful', and its philosophical texts so 'deep', because its philosophers are sufficiently abstract and equivocal in expression to be used in many unexpected and even mutually contradictory ways – *and the philosophers themselves do little or nothing to arrest that tendency.* They refuse to stand behind their own words in public. Not surprisingly, the words acquire a life of their own, as readers find it easy to treat their authors as dead. Of course, this attitude is quite consistent with a philosophical position that first burst on the scene 40 years ago by proclaiming 'the death of the author'.

Interlude: why breadth is better than depth

P: Maybe you're right about Butler and other continental philosophers. But I'm a little concerned about what might be your more general views about 'depth'. Surely there are some genuinely deep philosophical issues as well as some genuinely deep philosophical texts. **I:** You're right to be concerned! These 'deep' philosophical issues are merely questions that appear to arise over and over: What is the true? What is the good? What is the just? Of course, they're legitimate questions. And each time they're asked, different answers are given. But over time most of the differences are forgotten, and so they are repeatedly reinvented. Unfortunately philosophers are too easily impressed with the fact that the old problems always seem to generate the same range of solutions. This naïve attitude towards historical amnesia then produces the illusion of depth. As for 'deep' philosophical texts, well, here I am even more sceptical. Appeals to depth merely restrict the flow of intellectual traffic, as we saw with Butler.

P: I know – 'one-stop shopping for the mind'!

I: Indeed. My preference for breadth over depth is not simply based on the well-publicised excesses of continental philosophy. It is principled. One of the most disturbing and disappointing features of intellectual history is what economists would identify as its strong sense of 'path-dependency'. In other words, the arbitrariness with which certain texts become authoritative does not seem to stop them from anchoring entire fields of study for decades, sometimes even centuries. Thomas Kuhn called these intellectual anchors 'paradigms'. However, to a professional intellectual like myself, this practice has all the hallmarks of a superstition, a bit like the pious natives who justify their ritualised rain dances by recalling the major drought that ended after the very first dance. Of course, the more often these rain dances are done, the more they come to be bound up with other things that hold the tribe together, so the fact that the dances now rarely result in rain no longer seems so pressing. Academia is largely to blame for instituting a similarly superstitious attitude towards intellectual life.

P: Oh no, more academia bashing!

I: Hear me out! A genuine intellectual finds something fundamentally suspicious about the idea that there is only one or even a limited set of preferred routes to a truth of purportedly universal import: either this so-called truth is really a covert instrument of power that depends on restricted access or else, if it is really a universal truth, there are always other non-authorised ways of getting at it. Much of the public's ambivalence over science – as society's authorised producer, keeper and dispenser of truths – boils down to this suspicion. Thus, if a scientist insists on communicating in a jargon that cannot be fathomed without many years of concentrated study, then self-respecting members of the public may reasonably conclude that the scientist is either concealing her ignorance or revealing her contempt. In either case, they are entitled to call the scientist's bluff and request an alternative formulation. Anything worth saying can always be said in other words. This is how I get from depth to breadth. It appeals to my democratic sensibility, which refuses to believe that the wisdom of humanity is monopolised by the few people on whose words academics lavish attention and model their own discourses.

P: This still sounds to me like academia bashing.

I: Well, I have certainly not hidden my loathing of scholasticism. I don't see universities as primarily manufacturers of intellectual standards, let alone taste. That's the work of intellectuals, who may or may not be employed as academics. You might say that intellectuals consume academic research in order to produce a higher form of knowledge. Universities are like vineyards, academics like wine producers and intellectuals like connoisseurs. Wine producers justify their existence simply by producing wine that sells, whereas connoisseurs justify their existence by prescribing which wines should be drunk with which meals, if at all. More generally speaking, if we imagine society as a literal 'body politic', the work of intellectuals amounts to the digestive system that provides nutrition.

P: Enough analogies already! What role do you see, then, for universities in the intellectual world?

I: They are corporate investors in a wide range of ideas drawn from a narrow range of people. The results are typically very significant for society and even impressive in their own right, largely because of the power and capital at the disposal of universities. Nevertheless, universities do not hold a monopoly on intellectual investments. Professional intellectuals diversify their portfolios by drawing on an uncommon mix of sources – some academically respectable, some less so. Moreover, some academic sources are treated in rather unusual and not very respectable ways. This is the point of breadth: a requirement of our humanity is a principled willingness to give each person a fair hearing.

P: But you know as well as I do that this is impossible in practice.

I: So you say! Nevertheless, historically this is how the social sciences managed to define themselves against the élite bookishness of the humanities. Need I remind you that even today many people believe that more can be learned about the human condition by reading the Bible or Shakespeare than by talking to other human beings? The idea that all people matter – and matter equally – is not just a political principle but an epistemic one as well. Indeed, the social sciences are precisely what you get once academics start holding depth hostage to breadth. Why do you suppose already in the 18th century economists were interested in counting people and measuring their 'vital statistics' as population distributions? Why do you suppose by the late 19th century sociologists were going to ordinary people's homes to find out what they thought about their lives? And why do you suppose – now moving into the 20th century – political scientists were keen on capturing 'public opinion' through polls and surveys? All of these methods, diverse as they are, presuppose the value of authorising people to represent themselves in some fashion, even if only as a number in a social scientist's data sheet.

P: So, then, why aren't *you* a social scientist?

I: Unfortunately social scientists have been historically captive to their clients. To be sure, the distinctive methods of the social sciences had honourable origins as tools of great intellectual acuity. The intent was to challenge what had been taken for granted about the workings of society, especially the default status enjoyed by something called 'tradition'. Quantitative methods –

from statistics to experimental design – were developed in concert with attempts to think from first principles the fundamental categories and relations of social life. More qualitative methods – especially ethnographic techniques – were often indebted to investigative journalists wanting to 'get behind the scenes'. For example, this is how Friedrich Engels, as observer of working-class life in the great British industrial towns, provided some of his most valuable input to the Marxist project.

P: So what happened?

I: The social science findings typically became pawns in ongoing struggles among the parties who paid for the research to be done. Thus, the pioneers of statistical methods saw themselves as initiating a great conversation about alternative futures that could be extrapolated from current trends. However, they succeeded only in inspiring the design of large-scale systems of social control. Likewise, the muck-raking instincts of ethnographers came to be sublimated as 'deep cover' surveillance operations that enabled clients to intervene more strategically into the affairs of otherwise closed groups.

P: But surely you don't entirely disown the social sciences?

I: Of course not. In fact, my own work as an intellectual is parasitic on what social scientists do. Nevertheless, they enter into a Faustian bargain that I respectfully decline …

P: … but nonetheless take advantage of?

I: Precisely. For whatever reason, social scientists – like other academics – feel that access to more resources enables them to make their points more effectively. Thus, progress always seems to require larger and more representative samples of data studied for longer periods. I am here reminded of the Jorge Luis Borges story about the school of geographers whose proudest achievement was to have produced a map of the earth on a 1:1 scale. Too bad the map could never be unfolded and used! Suffice it to say, the more it costs to pursue knowledge, the more restricted the client base – though the relevance of the knowledge so produced may be as broad as ever. Generally speaking, unless a fiscally empowered state has stepped in as the public's agent, the social sciences have been used by the few to control the many in ever more ingenious – and usually less intrusive – ways.

P: If you truly believe this to have been the historical trajectory of the social sciences, then why don't you outright condemn these fields?

I: Well, we live in an imperfect world, and as a professional intellectual I don't have the philosopher's luxury of drawing a paycheque for being uniformly negative towards all established forms of inquiry. Students may take philosophy classes to be exposed to scepticism in this pure form, but the intellectual's lessons are taught by diluting scepticism in a solution of more sociable perspectives. Luckily, more knowledge is produced than can ever be used. In many cases this may even be deliberate, as social scientists comfort themselves with the prospect of serving two masters at once: the specific client who hands them a paycheque and a more diffuse community of readers who may draw on their work in quite unexpected ways.

P: And I suppose you include yourself among the latter?

I: Indeed. Here intellectuals can take heart from a phenomenon identified about twenty years ago by Don Swanson, a library scientist at the University of Chicago. He called it 'undiscovered public knowledge'. Swanson showed that standing problems in medical research may be significantly addressed, perhaps even solved, simply by systematically surveying the scientific literature. Left to its own devices, scientific research tends to become more specialised and abstracted from the real-world problems that motivated it and to which it remains relevant. This suggests that such a problem may be tackled effectively not by commissioning still more research, but by assuming that most or all of the solution can be already found in various scientific journals, waiting to be assembled by someone willing to read across specialities. Swanson himself did this in the case of Raynaud's Syndrome, a disease that causes the fingers of young women to become numb. His finding is especially striking – perhaps even scandalous – because it happened in the ever-expanding biomedical sciences. We take for granted that researchers who demand bigger research budgets have drawn all the insight they could from what others have done. But, according to Swanson, this is hardly the case.

P: So, how exactly does undiscovered public knowledge impact on the intellectual's livelihood?

I: Two ways. First, it emboldens intellectuals to question the extreme claims that academic researchers sometimes make in press releases and publishers' notices: is a finding truly novel or have we just forgotten a worthy precursor? Does solving an important problem really require massive additional funding or could a computerised search engine, creatively deployed, do the same job more quickly and cheaply? Second, and more positively, the existence of undiscovered public knowledge provides renewed legitimacy for the intellectual's omnivorous reading habits. Perhaps intellectuals concede too much when we cast ourselves as 'parasites' on original research. Rather we may be contributing to a sustainable research environment by making the most out of what is already available.

Of monuments and hypocrites: the case of analytic philosophers

P: We seem to have strayed a bit from our original remit. You have done a decent job of showing how intellectuals rise above the shortcomings of continental philosophers. However, I then let you veer into a more general critique of the excesses of academic institutions, what you call 'scholasticism', which you treated as a refined form of organised superstition. Even granting your central points – which I believe could benefit from more sustained scrutiny – I think you'll find it more difficult to defend yourself in the face of analytic philosophers. You cannot deny that these philosophers have made the most of drawing attention to distinctions that intellectuals like yourself are prone to blur in the heat of polemic.

I: I'm afraid I must disappoint you. Yes, analytic philosophers make much of drawing distinctions to clarify thought. But in practice they are given to distilling the details of complex arguments into a two-dimensional demonised opponent, especially when they lack specific knowledge of the opponent's position. The Village Sceptic and the Self-Refuting Relativist come to mind as two phantom interlocutors routinely conjured up these days to avoid having to deal with real social scientists. They are stock characters from the scholastic morality plays that analytic philosophers stage to intimidate first-year college students. In three lines of impeccable deductive reasoning, students are taught how to dismiss reams of impenetrable prose, typically of non-English provenance.

P: You ridicule this practice, but exactly what's wrong with it?

I: I suppose, in one sense, there is much for intellectuals to admire in what these philosophers – say, John Searle, Thomas Nagel, Daniel Dennett and Simon Blackburn – are capable of doing in the pages of the *New York Review of Books* and the *Times Literary Supplement*. Analytic philosophers share the intellectual's innate distrust of what I call *monumentalism*, that is, the idea that you can overpower an opponent by sheer force, be it political, economic or simply verbal – the number of long words and twisted sentences amassed on a page. If dominant beliefs are to be overturned, bigger must not always be better. It must be possible for a tightly budgeted line of reasoning to subvert high-maintenance bodies of thought. Otherwise, knowledge turns into a covert form of social stratification, just as that trainer of philosopher-kings, Plato, would have it.

P: I couldn't agree more. So then why pick on the analytic philosophers?

I: First of all, they're hypocrites, at least in their attitudes towards intellectuals. When I try to express myself simply and directly, I am accused of blurring crucial distinctions, stereotyping opponents and succumbing to deadline pressures. However, when they do exactly the same thing, it's called 'cutting through verbiage' and 'getting to the heart of the matter'. Truth be told, analytic philosophers and the readers of the *NYRB* and the *TLS* share attention spans of about the same length. Both start squirming in their seats if an argument lasts longer than about the 6,000 words of an article or the 60 minutes of a seminar. At that point, both suspect that obfuscation has got the upper hand on reason.

P: More insults!

I: No, it's a backhanded compliment! The anti-monumentalist impulse that keeps arguments short and sweet appeals to me. But I envy analytic philosophers the ease with which they can convert this impulse into the mark of a penetrative intellect, not mere impatience or, worse, laziness. (I can't count how many times I've been accused of such things – usually by people like you!) A more serious problem, however, is that analytic philosophers are not equal opportunity opponents of monumentalism. In fact, they often go out of their way to defend the most monumentalist form of knowledge of our times, the natural sciences.

P: Of course, analytic philosophy has been influenced by the problem-based nature of scientific inquiry, which requires a clear, even testable, formulation of knowledge claims. Surely you can't object to that. Indeed, it points to a genuine continuity between the histories of philosophy and science. It is easy to see that the problems physicists tackle about the relativity of space and time were originally addressed by Leibniz, that Kant still provides the template for debates over which aspects of our psychology are innate versus learned, and that recent Darwinian debates over the definition of species continue discussions originally launched by Aristotle.

I: Well, actually, that *is* the problem: the continuity between philosophy and science runs a bit too deep. They are effectively in each other's pockets. Analytic philosophers themselves often draw attention to this point, but they do not recognise its import. Philosophers frequently compliment scientists for adding some nuance to a set of issues that were first articulated by a philosopher, typically several centuries ago. Moreover, recent research often makes more sense of the old philosopher than his own contemporaries had appreciated.

P: Yes, but these things are sometimes true!

I: And you don't see the problem here? If the best defence that analytic philosophers can make of current scientific research is that it addresses age-old philosophical questions – but never quite answers them – why then does it cost so much more to do science than philosophy? Considering the cost of staffing and equipping laboratories, it routinely takes thousands, sometimes even millions, more dollars to do science than philosophy. And all this just to end up making minor improvements on some old philosophical discourse? I never cease to be amazed at the tolerance, if not indulgence, that analytic philosophers display towards scientific monumentalism.

P: You're entering dangerous ground here. Science is the one universally respected bulwark against the creeping forces of irrationalism in our civilisation.

I: And what might be these 'creeping forces'?

P: You know exactly what I'm talking about: Creationists, practitioners of New Age medicine, religious fundamentalists, postmodernists … I could go on.

I: I already get the idea. But I'm not sure how indulging science's monumentalist tendencies fights these creeping forces. Wouldn't it be smarter, strategically speaking, to call for a mass distribution of current scientific knowledge? Why encourage scientists to produce more knowledge that is likely to circulate only among those who can afford to train the relevant people to conduct the relevant specialised forms of research? Doesn't this simply increase the distance between science and the rest of society, making the latter more susceptible to the dark forces of unreason?

P: There are two answers to your questions. First, you're working with a false dichotomy. Just because analytic philosophers don't normally talk about the need to impose science on the curriculum, it doesn't follow that they wouldn't support such a move. The advancement of science needs to proceed on many fronts at once. At the same time, however, analytic philosophers may be a bit reluctant to support such a move explicitly because they wouldn't want to be seen as encouraging the formation of a new dogma. After all, the main reason analytic philosophers tend to think that scientists make only marginal progress on the old philosophers is that scientists still fail to address the most fundamental sceptical queries of their positions.

I: Now I'm totally confused. It sounds to me as if analytic philosophers support science only out of expedience.

P: Well, philosophy remains the best way to address problems relating to the ultimate nature of reality. However, people have mixed motives for asking deep questions. In that respect, philosophy may not be sufficient to their needs. They may wish to do something – shall we say, more 'productive' – with their lives …

I: … You mean they want to be sufficiently committed

to a set of beliefs to try to realise them in a sustained piece of work that then manages to impress even those who lack those beliefs? After all, most of the people who walk across a bridge know nothing of the physical principles that inspired its design, yet still they walk – and live to tell of the experience. That sense of authority over people's lives must be a source of personal satisfaction to the person who designed the bridge.

P: Yes, I suppose that's one way of putting it. Science often satisfies that need in people, certainly more soundly than alternative lines of work. Nevertheless, the best scientists respect philosophy sufficiently to be modest in their ultimate conclusions. In return, philosophers could do much worse than encourage the work of such scientists.

I: I appreciate the candour of your response, but it reveals just how little analytic philosophers have themselves progressed from Plato! You have basically provided a justification for stratifying society on the basis of knowledge. You neither trust scientists enough to have them take over your philosophical functions nor trust non-scientists enough to have them discover science's shortcomings for themselves. It is as if your invocation of the great philosophical precursors is designed to immunise both scientists against dogmatism and non-scientists against scepticism.

P: And is that such a bad bargain to strike in today's unstable world?

I: Well, yes! Analytic philosophers neglect the political and economic costs of their diplomatic manoeuvres. Perhaps the most incontrovertible trend in the history of the sciences is that the march of progress corresponds to the consumption of greater resources, which in turn produces greater impacts on the rest of society. The state, as the guarantor of human rights and civil society, fights an increasingly uphill battle to regulate both of these gargantuan tendencies.

P: True, but here clarity may be gained by some time-honoured philosophical distinctions, such as pure versus applied research, fact versus value, and, indeed, science versus politics.

I: 'Time-honoured' gives the game away. These distinctions are largely *nostalgic* in the full sense of harking back to a mythical past.

P: How so?

I: Consider 'fact versus value'. Nowadays this distinction looks like a division of labour: scientists produce knowledge ('facts') and the public decides what to do with it ('values'). However, the distinction was introduced only when scientists no longer had exclusive control over the use of the knowledge they produced. This happened once the conduct of science had reached such a scale that the cost of its maintenance forced scientists to solicit funds from outside sources. These sources – both state and industry – are interested in science for their own reasons, which are not necessarily those of the scientists themselves. Consequently, scientists learn a kind of doublespeak that enables them – at least to their own satisfaction – to serve truth and power at once. They imagine that theorists and practitioners are different people, just as the blackboard and the lab bench are in different rooms.

P: I have yet to see the problem.

I: The 'problem', such as it is, lies in the irony of history. The US Congress was persuaded to create the National Science Foundation after the Second World War because the masterminds behind the construction of the first successful atomic bomb had been some of the original theorists of atomic energy. This was definitive proof – at least for politicians – that a detour through intellectual abstractions can be the shortest route to practical results. No more self-made men like Edison and Ford – bring on the doctors of physics marching lockstep behind Einstein and Bohr!

P: I really think it's inappropriate to judge the soundness of philosophical distinctions by whether they make life easy for politicians and industrialists.

I: It's not just the people who pay scientists who don't believe in the dichotomies you've conjured up. Nor do the sociologists who study scientists empirically in their research sites. Indeed, the sociology of science would not be such a controversial field today – the site of the so-called Science Wars – if scientists either lived up to their philosophical hype or simply learned to tone it down. In this respect, the sociologists are merely the messengers blamed for the bad news. Only the scientists themselves, buoyed by analytic philosophers, uphold the illusory distinctions you champion. This, in turn, only serves to distance scientists from the consequences of their actions so as to obscure their accountability to the public.

The final solution? Metaphysics as the higher ventriloquism

P: Even after all this storm and fury, I stand by my original charge: you intellectuals so reduce the complexity of the issues you raise that you undermine your stated aim of speaking truth to power.

I: Even if you're right, it doesn't follow that the sort of complexity you philosophers and other academics champion redresses matters. Philosophers should be on our side, but you always seem reluctant to assert in the face of uncertainty. Indeed, you would rather wish uncertainty away or project your voice onto a more certain version of reality.

P: What on earth could you mean by all that?

I: In a word: *metaphysics*, the last refuge of intellectual scoundrels. Metaphysicians are like ventriloquists afraid, incapable or unwilling to speak in their own voice. Thus, they manufacture entities that can convey their message incognito. These entities are then organised into a realm of being, or 'ontology', that might be quite elaborate and stratified. The ontology functions as a kind of virtual reality, or model, over which the philosopher can exert some nominal control – unlike the reality in which she normally dwells. Plato and his followers are the past masters of this sort of activity. Platonism has been generally attractive to those who see themselves as living in times promising little chance or point of challenging the way things are. Metaphysically fortified, Platonists reinforce the status quo by superimposing an additional level of meaning on, say, the class divisions or disciplinary distinctions that are already recognised. Of course, more ingenious Platonists have tried to double-code their ontologies, allowing for a 'hidden order' that eludes the powers that be. However, down this route lay esotericism, gnosticism and other cultish formations that are repugnant to the public-spiritedness of intellectuals.

P: I find it incredibly cavalier that you would write off all of metaphysics – the foundational discipline of philosophy – simply on the basis of some Platonic excesses!

I: OK, there is one kind of metaphysics that I believe can help the intellectual – but you won't like to hear about it.

P: No, I'm dying to find out!

I: *Reductionism!*

P: I'm sorry to disappoint you, but your endless desire to provoke has merely revealed your ignorance of the history of philosophy. Reductionism is itself a version of the cultish kind of Platonism you just disparaged. What do you suppose inspired the atomic theory of matter – the basis of the weird entities that currently populate modern physics? You forget that esoteric cults need not be confined to a few people hovering over a sacred text – hundreds milling around a particle accelerator may also qualify!

I: My God, you're beginning to sound like me! In any case, I don't mean *that* kind of reductionism. I mean the exact opposite, the kind that aims to 'reduce' all knowledge claims to a common evaluative medium, such as ordinary experience, logic or some combination of the two. In other words, I mean the sort of reductionism the logical positivists championed when they insisted that everything be 'verified' – and Karl Popper later said 'falsified'. These philosophers realised that a claim to knowledge is always a claim to authority, which means that if you claim to know something, you are requesting my deference to your authority. In response, I require that you first pass a mutually agreeable test. This may consist of an experiment, an interrogation or some other kind of examination. The point is that even the most grandiose or subtle of knowledge claims must always be expressible in terms such that even a reasonable non-expert might be persuaded. This exactly captures the intellectual's preferred field of play.

P: How so?

I: This kind of reductionism places the burden of proof on the person who would replace the interlocutor's epistemic authority with her own. Grounds for intellectual colonisation should never be presumed but must always be earned – ideally, case-by-case, individual-by-individual. Of course, expedience may force us to settle for less. We only have so much time to scrutinise each other's knowledge claims. But this regrettable fact should never be pumped up with metaphysical gas as, say, 'trustworthy witness' or 'reliable testimony', in which the double negative of 'failure to find error' is wishfully converted into a positive 'truth'. The refusal to inquire further into some matter should always be treated as a free choice, whose consequences the refuser then takes responsibility for.

P: Aren't you proposing a rather harsh intellectual ethic?

I: Well, I never said being an intellectual was easy.

P: But would you make all of metaphysics up for grabs in this fashion – reducing it to whatever tests the parties can agree upon for their knowledge claims? Is there nothing that all parties to such tests would agree simply *must* be the case?

I: When philosophers talk about what 'must' be the case, they sound like they are saying something deep about the logical or physical structure of the actual world. However, on closer inspection, they often turn out to be making a political or moral statement about how they would like the world to be – but has yet to become. Of course, there's nothing wrong with articulating one's hopes and dreams. Richard Rorty, the national philosopher of the United States, is refreshingly honest on this score. You may not like where he's trying to go, but at least you know where he's coming from. Rorty appeals directly to the moral superiority of the American liberal tradition to justify his vision of the good society. He does not hide behind transcendental arguments, stratified ontologies and question-begging definitions. The force of arguing what *must* be the case is that open intellectual debate about the desirability of the claims is pre-empted. One is simply made to appear irrational, if one fails to see what the philosopher declares to be true 'by necessity'.

P: What you've been talking about here reminds me of what we philosophers call the *deontic fallacy*. In English and other languages, words that are meant to modify something's state of being (or 'modalities') like 'must' and 'necessary' (as well as 'can' and 'possible') can be understood in two distinct ways: as part of the vocabulary of either ethics and law or logic and science. The sense of obligation or compulsion imposed in the two types of cases is rather different and may even work at cross-purposes. For example, the Mosaic Commandment 'Thou shalt not kill' does not say that committing murder is conceptually or physically impossible. On the contrary, it presupposes that murder is all too possible. Thus, murder needs to be prohibited by the norms of society, subject to severe punishment. This is a good example of the two senses of 'must' and 'can' cutting against each other in just the right way. It also seems to capture the sensibility you said – at the start of this dialogue – joins intellectuals and scientists in common cause …

I: … Yes, we do not slavishly capitulate to the contours of reality.

P: However, you now appear to be spinning the deontic fallacy the other way round to make philosophers its unwitting victims. If I understand you correctly, you hold that what philosophers call 'metaphysics' is nothing but an illicit projection of their fantasies onto the contours of reality. I find that hard to believe. Notwithstanding your earlier remarks about analytic philosophers, it seems to me that it is you who are resorting to straw men here. Exactly which philosophers are you talking about?

I: Lots of them, I'm afraid. With an eye to our old friend Judith Butler, the literary critic Jonathan Dollimore has coined the phrase 'wishful theory' for self-declared 'radical' academics who regard the clearing of conceptual space as *ipso facto* a bold political gesture. For example, if you strip Butler's argument of its Francophile packaging, you get something like this: because it is logically and physically possible for a man to pass as a woman – and vice versa – it follows that society generally permits these cross-gender manoeuvres, which in turn can be deployed to undermine forms of oppression based on a rigid sense of sexual difference. Only someone whose life resembles that of the abstract possibility in the premise of this argument – that one is oppressed *only* at the level of sexual (and not also, say, race or class) difference – could find what Butler says remotely persuasive. Her queer theory is, as advertisers say of élite gifts, 'for the person who has everything'.

P: But we've already agreed that Butler is an extreme case who appeals to an élite constituency. It's unfair to tar all philosophers with the same brush of 'wishful theory'.

I: Is it so unfair? In the end, I agree, Butler's wishful theory is little more than a bourgeois American utopia. You'll recall, however, that when I raised the topic of metaphysics, I focused on 'must', not 'can', as the operative word. Something much more sinister is going on in that case.

P: You already said that philosophers who base their arguments on what 'must' be true end up prohibiting dissent. However, I find it hard to imagine that any contemporary philosophers could exert that level of control over intellectual life.

I: I suspect the problem here is that you imagine the prohibition of dissent always comes from a position of strength. But my point is that it usually comes from a position of *weakness*. Appeals to what must be the case typically aim to immunise a group of like-minded people against the temptation to change their minds. The invocation of some deep causal structure or inexorable law is designed to ward off any inconvenient facts. Such facts are then demoted to mere appearances or systematically distorted interpretations of reality.

P: I can see how a millenarian religious cult might resort to this strategy, once the apocalypse fails to materialise according to plan. But how could philosophers be found guilty of this particular intellectual sin?

I: Just look at the recent spate of analytic philosophers who call themselves and their positions *realist*. As the name suggests, these philosophers are above all committed to a belief in an ultimate reality that underwrites all that is true and towards which all our inquiries, despite their surface differences, are necessarily directed. At the very least, then, a providential view of history is implicated. (Need I mention that the realist ranks are full of disenchanted Christians and Marxists?) Yet realists also don't wish to commit themselves to any particular truths. Even ordinary empirical regularities might be explained as temporary diversions or distortions. Thus, realists like to observe that for 2,000 years, Europeans believed that Aristotle's earth-centred view of the cosmos was largely correct because their evidence base was rather skewed, itself the result of what we can now see to have been theoretical biases and limited instruments.

P: I have yet to see the problem here. On the contrary, I would have thought that you as the relentlessly inquisitive intellectual would count yourself among the realists. Don't you relish the opportunity to unmask the long-standing errors of others?

I: Yes, but I also like to take responsibility for having done so – and am happy to pay the price of exposing myself to criticism if I am later shown not to have done so. Metaphysics just gets in the way! All that is needed is a socially constructed and mutually recognised standard of evaluation, a court in which I can stand trial. Give me that and I might just move the world!

FREQUENTLY ASKED QUESTIONS ABOUT INTELLECTUALS

What is the intellectual's attitude towards ideas?

Intellectuals have understood ideas along two dimensions, both of which are concerned with the relationship between an idea and its material container, be it a brain, a book, a databank or an entire society. For the sake of convenience, let's call these two dimensions *ancient* and *modern*.

The poles of the *ancient* dimension are represented by the Greek philosophers Plato and Aristotle. Plato believed that ideas are always trying to escape their material containers to return to some pristine state of unity with all the other ideas in heaven. In contrast, Aristotle held that ideas are involved in a different sort of struggle, namely, to provide their material containers with some form and purpose, which in turn would bring the ideas to fruition. Plato's ideas are ethereal, Aristotle's seminal.

When intellectuals – usually philosophers – have longed for a frictionless medium of thought capable of pursuing ideas in all their possible combinations without the distractions of everyday life, including one's own body, they have adopted Plato's point of view. A version of this view can be found even among lawyers and economists who uphold the naturally fugitive character of ideas, which then places the burden of proof on those who would make claims to 'intellectual property', an oxymoron to the Platonist. However, this burden is gladly borne by the Aristotelian, who believes that both idea and matter achieve full realisation only when combined. This mentality has been operative in many of the key concepts of Western civilisation, ranging from sacred ideas that grant humans dominion over the earth to more secular ones that peg the value of material goods to the labour invested in their production. In each case, ideas infuse life into an otherwise inert matter.

The poles of the *modern* dimension of ideas are metaphors borrowed from two natural sciences, physics and biology. In both cases, ideas are understood as a dynamic feature of matter. At the physics end, ideas are radioactive. They are parts of existent matter, which upon escape can contaminate and even produce new things, some of which may be deadly upon contact. But for these mutants to be lethal, you must first interact with them, which typically means an explicit interest on your part, say, in new sources of nuclear energy. The radioactive mutants are not trying to find you. On the other hand, at the biology end, ideas are parasites always in search of new hosts. These parasites threaten to contaminate and perhaps even overwhelm you. Whereas radioactive ideas can be simply avoided altogether, the

unavoidable nature of parasitic ideas requires that
potential hosts be immunised against their worst effects.

We see, then, two opposing roles for the intellectual:
the censor who prohibits the cultivation of certain ideas
and the devil's advocate who exposes people to ideas she
hopes will be accepted in a mild form, which then
enables them to reject the more virulent forms. The
censor and the devil's advocate capture the natural place
of intellectuals in, respectively, authoritarian and democratic regimes.

Do intellectuals display any characteristic speech patterns?

Intellectuals talk about abstractions as if they were
land-masses, arguments and ideas as strategies and
tactics. Only an intellectual would say something like
'Capitalism will be overcome by class struggle' or
'Gender domination will be subverted by placing the
male-female distinction under erasure' – and then give
you a puzzled look if you ask exactly how to go about
doing this. Nevertheless, thinking is a kind of fighting.
Indeed, the Greeks used the language of 'dialectics' to
cover both activities. The intellectual needs positions,
preferably defined in opposition to each other, as in the
case of 'left' and 'right' or 'progressive' and 'reactionary'.
Thus, the repeated attempts to proclaim 'the end of
ideology' over the past half-century drive a stake through
the intellectual's heart.

Intellectuals also betray a fondness for words like 'mentality', 'sensibility', 'attitude', 'mood', 'mindset', 'standpoint', 'worldview', 'bias', 'prejudice' and, of course, 'ideology'. These words share certain characteristics. They are all second-order terms relating to ideas. They don't refer to specific ideas but rather to kinds of ideas that are presumed to be organised and oriented towards something else. The ideas themselves are pawns, tokens or signs in a largely implicit relationship between the subject who possesses the ideas and the objects towards which they are directed.

For example, when an intellectual accuses someone of being a 'capitalist', she is not saying that the person believes in the truth of a fixed set of propositions, as an especially flat-footed philosopher might think. Rather, the intellectual means that whatever the person believes – the actual propositions may be rather vague and variable – is geared towards maintaining a certain 'capitalistic' way of being in the world. A judgement of this sort can be made only after observing the person's actions in many contexts and taking her words as symptoms, but not necessarily mirrors, of her true motivation. Thus, the person may claim to be a devout Christian who regularly attributes her success to Divine Grace yet, in practice, turns out to value people, actions and things in proportion to their market values. Such a person is a capitalist, in spite of herself.

How do you acquire credibility as an intellectual?

You basically need to demonstrate your independence of thought, what Immanuel Kant called *autonomy*. Autonomy is most effectively conveyed by being 'cast against type', as actors say. In other words, you should adopt positions that do not seem to be in your interest to uphold. When the great sociologist of knowledge Karl Mannheim called the intelligentsia 'free-floating', he meant just this: intellectuals appear detached from their socio-economic moorings. The more mysterious the benefit you would receive from the truth of your position, the more intellectual integrity you will appear to have. Of course, it does not follow that people will entrust you with their lives or even come round to your point of view. But then those are not the measures of your success. Instead you should seek to plant a chronic nagging doubt in your audience, which causes them to leave your speech or text thinking, 'She must have a point; why else would she say these crazy things?' This means you have shifted the burden of proof, ever so slightly, in favour of a less popular position.

It is relatively easy to demonstrate autonomy if you come from a wealthy or aristocratic background. You simply need to disown your status and champion the poor and downtrodden. It worked for the Buddha, and it enabled socialism to gain a political foothold long before it became a proper workers' movement. Moreover, this strategy may even help socialism survive long after the workers have abandoned the movement in search of middle-class identities. (Socialism's most steadfast defender in the UK over the past half-century has been the aristocrat Anthony Wedgwood Benn, better known as Tony Benn.) The strategy typically involves denouncing the corrupt conditions that maintain your status. Your discovery of this corruption turns out to be an unintended consequence of the superior education and leisure you illicitly enjoy. You then dedicate the rest of your life to undoing the inequities, in part to atone for your own complicity in them.

Autonomy is much harder to demonstrate if you come from a poor or proletarian background. On the one hand, calls to end poverty are undoubtedly well taken but also clearly self-serving. On the other hand, calls to join the wealthy in common cause appear to betray one's class origins. To get beyond this impasse, the impoverished intellectual must engage in what the social phenomenologist Max Scheler called 'the manufacture of ideals'. Ideals are manufactured by inverting the presumed value structure, so that one openly courts what is normally avoided. Poverty thus becomes a source of hidden wealth, and the proletariat's expressive shortcomings metamorphose into an untapped reservoir of 'popular culture'. The basic idea is that one converts an apparent liability into a subtle virtue, what the political theorist Jon Elster has called 'sweet lemons', the converse of 'sour grapes'.

This strategy worked for Jesus and explains much of the success of Christianity. However, it works only if the value inversion turns out to be an indirect means of realising the normal value structure. For example, the poor and the rich may be portrayed as mutually alienated siblings, neither of whom can realise their full potential without recognising their forgotten common ancestor. In Biblical terms, the meek must end up inheriting the earth in a manner that commands the respect of the strong. A failed version of this strategy is the Newspeak that features in Orwell's *Nineteen Eighty-four*, where the prevailing misery is consistently given such an uplifting gloss that oppression is renamed 'freedom'. Those who complain about 'political correctness' in the reform of academia – and society more generally – have just this sort of precedent in mind, where only the names have changed and the world remains the same. In such cases, intellectuals have literally lost the plot. As a safeguard, the intellectual must resist the narcissistic impulse to embrace the fetishism of the word that so often passes for the institutionalisation of the deed.

However, if the intellectual manages to have her own ideas institutionalised, she should be supportive without trying to micro-manage the supporters' efforts or appearing ungrateful at the results. A true intellectual is bored by the routine character of institutionalisation, which is better left to those with the requisite patience and humility. Moreover, history teaches that playing an active role in the implementation of your ideas too often resembles presiding over the murder of your children. Ask any intellectual who became a commissar.

Nevertheless, the intellectual cannot remain completely aloof, as if her ideas were bottled messages en route to some unknown destination. You must remain cognisant of the difference between people invoking your ideas or your name in ways you simply failed to anticipate and in ways you actually oppose. The latter situation morally requires your intervention, even if you think that your sway over your constituency extends no further than the moment they hear your words. Silence would constitute a failure of intellectual responsibility of the highest order.

How does an intellectual choose a cause to champion?

Intellectuals champion ideas that reconfigure groups, scramble the political field. They discover hidden constituencies whose memberships cut across conventional social boundaries. These are then turned into 'ideas'. It is here that intellectuals differ most clearly from conventional politicians, ideologues or lobbyists – all of whom represent groups that already possess clear identities and interests by virtue of formal membership or residence. The original intellectuals of the Enlightenment tried to appeal across societal differences by transcending them in the name of ideas that they thought could command universal allegiance – most notably the abstractions Liberty, Equality and Fraternity that inspired the French Revolution of 1789. The Christian roots of this strategy were obvious at the time and became explicit in the next generation's fixation on the Religion of Humanity, or Positivism, the secular philosophical form in which it was known for most of the 19th and 20th centuries. Positivism's chequered legacy is that the scientific establishment today enjoys the sort of authority that half a millennium earlier would have been the preserve of the Roman Catholic Church.

However, most ideas championed by intellectuals have been more mid-range – not about humanity as a whole but only a part of it. An idea of this sort causes people to think about themselves in novel ways, perhaps drawing on aspects of their ancestors' lives that have been largely forgotten or suppressed though they continue to survive in a vestigial form. This remembrance of things past is designed to enable the intellectual's target audience to redistribute the meaning they invest in the various aspects of their own lives. The Zionist movement exemplifies this strategy. Theodor Herzl's biggest challenge in the late 19th century was to convince assimilated European Jews that their Jewishness was worth resurrecting as a primary marker of their identity. Generally speaking, and certainly in the case of Zionism, the redistributions of meaning urged by intellectuals generate new social divisions. This is simply another way of talking about 'politicisation'.

Market researchers are grunt-level intellectuals who are contracted to find things ordinary people care about by conducting focus groups. They then repackage what the people say as ideas that can be sold to politicians as the basis for legislation or to business for new products. These just-in-time intellectuals may even serve double duty, especially in today's universities, where an increasing proportion of researchers are on short-term contracts. Thus, the public's worries about environmental hazards have been commodified as the 'risk society'. This then generates several parallel capital streams, as the phrase simultaneously inspires a new domain of academic investigation, a plank in a political party platform and, not least, a new line of upmarket consumer goods.

'Liberty, Equality, Fraternity': which matters the most to the intellectual?

Of course, all three matter. However, strange as it may seem, *fraternity* matters most of all. To be sure, contemporary political theorists pass over fraternity in embarrassed silence because of its sexist roots. At most 'fraternity' conveys a warm glow from the dying embers of socialism but no discernible content. To recover the significance of fraternity for the intellectual, we need to root around the concept's unfashionable ancestry in Christianity.

Fraternity is based on the idea that even if we do not have the same biological parent, we still share a more profound ancestor, whose recognition should lead us to join in common cause. In Christianity, this is of course God the Father, but the secular variants are equally powerful to call forth the activity of the intellectual. When Jesus instructed his disciples to leave their families and forge new social bonds capable of indefinite expansion in the name of spreading the gospel, he was making quite a revolutionary proposal. His target audience, fellow Jews, had become Jews simply by birth into a Jewish family. Yet here was one of their own who claimed that what privileges us as human beings in the precise sense of Holy Scripture – 'born in the image and likeness of God' – has nothing to do with biology. (What would a travelling Darwinist have made of all this?!) Thus, the great Christian proselytisers have been 'born again' like St Paul and St Augustine, people who very publicly disowned their material origins to become bearers of a certain set of ideas.

This sensibility has had profound repercussions in the history of the West, principally through Roman law. Although Christianity becomes the official religion of the Roman Empire in the 4th century AD, another seven centuries must pass before Jesus' message is properly institutionalised. Roman law traditionally defined individuals in one of two ways. The default position was as a family member, be it noble or peasant. This is what we normally mean by 'feudalism', the stereotypical vision of the Middle Ages. However, sometimes individuals from different family backgrounds would form temporary alliances for specific ends, such as a mission of religious conversion or a foreign business venture. You then enjoyed legal protection for the duration of these typically violent activities (e.g. crusades, piracy). But upon the activity's conclusion – assuming you were still alive – you reverted to your family-based status.

The key innovation for intellectuals – the one that established a distinctively spiritual sense of 'fraternity' – was what the Romans called *universitas*, which is normally translated in English as 'corporation'. However, business firms were relative latecomers to the legal status of corporation, as illustrated by the persistence of family names in the business world. The original corporations were guilds, churches, city-states, and of course universities. What entitled all of them to that artificial birth certificate – the corporate charter – is a sense of purpose that extends beyond the interests and even lifetimes of the individuals who happen to be its current members. For example, a guild is dedicated to the cultivation of skills that can be the basis of a trade. However, these skills are passed down not by inheritance but by apprenticeship. The replacement of preordained succession by periodic election and examination across the entire range of social life has remained humanity's most effective means of transcending its animal origins on behalf of a set of ideas, or an *ideal*, that all of its members might share.

However, we should not confer too much other-worldliness on ideals, lest we end up with such self-defeating aberrations as the cult of celibacy and other gnostic attempts to act as if humanity rises above its biological nature by the sheer denial of it. What is really involved here is a non-biological form of human association that bears fruit in perpetuity through legal midwifery. Over time, the people involved in these associations come to identify more strongly with the artificially incorporated entity they help to create and maintain than with the natural entities from which they descended. Take an idea as concrete as the nation-state, a corporate entity that really comes into its own only in the 19th century but remains to this day the default site of collective political action. Constitutional conventions played a decisive role in determining how people of disparate backgrounds were to be converted into citizens of a new nation-state.

The idea of the nation-state seems quite ordinary now, perhaps even passé, but it had to be forged as an idea. The crucible turns out to have been the university, which in medieval times threw together students from the same region into residence halls known as *nationes*. Here the students constituted themselves as an interest group for university governance. This limited exercise in collective political identity often served as a dress rehearsal for the exercise of power in their homelands, as the students came to reconceptualise their arbitrary collocation in terms of a common project pursued not merely on campus but in perpetuity by successive generations of people just as arbitrarily collected in a much larger space – that is, a nation-state.

As nation-states began to coalesce in the modern period, these student unions took on a more subversive quality, a hotbed for conspiracy among élites in exile. Now the fraternal 'comrades' were united in replacing the old national ideal with a new revolutionary one. It is natural to associate this development with broadly socialist or post-colonial politics, but its roots are in the much derided 'frats' still found on US college campuses. The original fraternity, Phi Beta Kappa, was chartered at the College of William and Mary, the first training ground for colonial administrators in British America. Yet, within a century of its founding, the College had graduated Thomas Jefferson and other intellectuals behind the American Revolution. More to the point, the fraternity covertly supported the cause of independence by providing shelter for republican soldiers and their French allies in their self-governing 'frat houses'. This was not lost on the revolutionaries back in France who a decade later included 'fraternity' as the third term in their battle cry.

Are there different types of intellectuals? If so, how do you classify them?
Intellectuals may be contrasted along five dimensions.

1. How does being an intellectual fit into the person's career?
Some do it to make their name, others after they've made their name. The existence of both types casts doubt on the idea that inquiry must always be specialised, though

equally both are seen as exploiting the work of specialists. The former, typically journalists and freelance
writers, take advantage of hard-working but relatively
anonymous academics and experts. The latter use their
own relatively narrow expertise as a launch pad for
universalist claims, usually in aid of left-wing or counter-
cultural causes. Bertrand Russell (a logician), Albert
Einstein (a physicist), Noam Chomsky (a linguist) and
Edward Said (a literary critic) are 20th-century exemplars of this type. It is common to criticise this group
as merely 'trading' (i.e. 'coasting') on their academic
authority, though closer inspection reveals that the
character of their general claims and arguments bears
the marks of their original expertise. But behind such
churlish criticism may be the worry that truly inquiring
minds might not find the cultivation of specialist
knowledge sufficient for a satisfying intellectual life.

2. What is the source of the intellectual's appeal?

Some are *constituency-based*, others *client-driven*. In the
former case, the intellectual's ideas help to consolidate
the identity of a group that previously had only a latent
existence, whereas in the latter case, the intellectual's
ideas migrate across already existing groups, as the
opportunity arises. Intellectuals on opposite poles of this
dimension stake their claim to autonomy on rather
different grounds. Constituency-based intellectuals point
to the constitutive role of their ideas in uniting disparate
individuals in common cause, whereas client-driven

intellectuals refer to the ability of their ideas to serve many masters, including those who would otherwise be at loggerheads. Constituency-based intellectuals can be found among the purveyors of 'identity politics', whereas client-driven intellectuals dwell in think-tanks and consultancies.

The stylistic difference between these two types of intellectuals is most marked at the extremes, even when they cohabit the same university. Take two Berkeley-based intellectuals, the celebrated queer theorist Judith Butler and the guru of the 'informational society', Manuel Castells. At one extreme, Butler cloaks her ideas in esoteric jargon that erects a clear boundary between those inside and outside the chosen constituency; at the other extreme, Castells presents his protean ideas as a collage of cut-and-paste executive summaries of research conducted for an assortment of clients by many, typically lower status, associates. A lingering question is what will remain of the reputation of these intellectuals, once the constituency or client base loses its sociological salience. In the specific cases of Butler and Castells, what happens once gender-switching is no longer taboo and computer networks are fully integrated into the global economy?

3. How directly exposed is the intellectual's judgement to current events?
Some are *weathervanes* whose perspective is dictated by the terms of the immediate environment, others *echo*

chambers who continually translate the quotidian into the perennial. Weathervanes are blessed with an uncanny ability to see six months into the future, no more and no less. Their credibility rests on repeatedly displaying this ability. Otherwise, they might be confused with 'mere' journalists. This means a rapid succession of short books, each declaring what the intellectual (now) regards as the emergent tendency from processes (often the same ones) that have been gestating from time immemorial. A weathervane's career retrospective may prove the source of considerable embarrassment, especially if one associates an intellectual's autonomy with perseverance in the face of change. At the same time, however, the texts of such a fickle mind are likely to be among the most useful to historians. Indeed, the intellectual may acquire the posthumous reputation of having been 'sensitive' and 'responsive' for qualities that her contemporaries regarded as 'facile' and 'mercurial'.

The great British weathervane of our times is John Gray, Professor of European Thought at the London School of Economics. Gray first came to prominence in the 1980s as a champion of the Thatcherite icon, the Austrian economist Friedrich Hayek. Once the Labour Party was returned to power in the 1990s, Gray shifted ground and warned against the excesses of the free market and corporate globalisation. In the first decade of the new millennium, a period that combines disillusion with Labour and a renewed awareness of religious fundamentalism, Gray has come to blame the world's political and more general environmental problems on the West's modernist pretensions, which privilege human welfare over that of the rest of the planet. Today's Gray has been born again as a latter-day Gulliver, whose new-found love of 'deep ecology' leads him to prefer the company of the noble horses, the Houyhnhnms, to the grunt-like humans, the Yahoos. One wonders: is there a point when the intellectual weathervane's trajectory has become so buffeted by vicissitude that her cosmopolitan sensitivity shades into misanthropic disorientation?

All of this is in marked contrast to the sociologically inscrutable echo chamber intellectuals. They inhabit a world of virtual interlocutors who communicate across centuries on topics of perennial concern, in what Gray's own LSE precursor, Michael Oakeshott, dubbed 'the conversation of mankind'. The grandmaster of this genre in recent times has been Leo Strauss, a Jewish émigré from Nazi Germany who taught at the University of Chicago until the 1970s. Strauss himself was the author of many commentaries, mostly on European political thought before the Enlightenment, in which he attempted to demonstrate, over and over, that metaphysics simultaneously provides a secular cosmology for the pious and a political blueprint for the cunning. According to Strauss, philosophers since Plato have engaged in this doubletalk as an exercise in self-restraint, since only élite inquirers can grasp esoteric truths of universal significance without succumbing to the temptation to demystify a world whose very stability rests on mass illusion. Flattered by his esoteric message, Strauss' students make up the current crop of 'neo-conservatives' who populate the US civil service and government advisory posts. The message finally went public as the best-selling non-fiction book of 1987, *The Closing of the American Mind*, written by the Straussian Allan Bloom, the American translator of Plato's *Republic*.

4. How does your place in history define your role as an intellectual?

Crudely put: are you a *winner* or a *loser*? In terms familiar to historians of the English Civil War, are you a *Whig* who rides the wave of history and expresses its defining tendency, or a *Tory* who has been left behind to view events from a more detached perspective? Of course, you can win or lose in several ways. However, generally speaking, it is harder to retain your integrity as an intellectual if you pose as one of history's winners, since you will always be open to the charge of being a mere mouthpiece for the dominant ideology.

Two 20th-century figures who continue to be dogged by the 'mouthpiece' characterisation are the philosophers György Lukács and Martin Heidegger, who were unreconstructed supporters of Stalin and Hitler respectively. Their not entirely successful strategies for maintaining their autonomy were interestingly different. Lukács, who had begun his career as a bourgeois aesthetician, claimed to have undergone a Pauline conversion to Communism upon Lenin's victory in the 1917

Russian Revolution. We witness here an intellectual's attempt to establish credibility by being cast against type. In contrast, Heidegger consistently gave the appearance that Hitler's rise provided independent corroboration – though ultimately imperfect expression – of the dark ideas he had been expounding in his graduate seminars over the previous decade.

However, it is much easier for the intellectual simply to be left behind by history, a fate that can then be presented as a blessing in disguise. The founder of objective historiography in the Western tradition, Thucydides, is the patron saint of this approach. He so botched his stint as a general in the Athenian army in the Peloponnesian Wars that he was sent into exile, which allowed him to mix with the Spartans who fought Athens. The result was a masterpiece of sustained critical reflection on historical events rarely matched today. Thucydides' *The Peloponnesian Wars* remains the standard source for understanding the larger geopolitical context into which the original disputes between Socrates and the sophists played.

As a rule, nations that have been major military losers – the once mighty who have met an ignominious end – are the breeding grounds for this species of intellectual, who quite understandably have grown to distrust local authorities. If you recall that Poland and Hungary were the largest countries in late medieval Europe, you can see this immediately. Hegel's generation, the fount of German idealism and the start of modern academic culture, always harked back to the Prussian army's surrender to Napoleon at Jena in 1806. And, of course, the more France has been politically humiliated on the world stage, the more intellectuals it has spawned. In recent times, it has become possible to be a historical loser by more indirect means: your *raison d'être* might simply disappear. Step forward Francis Fukuyama, one of the many 'Sovietologists' working for the US State Department who had to find new jobs in the early 1990s. The blessing he found in disguise was that the Soviet Union turned out to be the final obstacle to the triumph of liberal democracy, or so it seemed in 1992, when *The End of History and the Last Man* was published.

5. Where exactly do intellectuals find the ideals they defend?
Some intellectuals defend an absent ideal and others the status quo. Those who defend an absent ideal may not explicitly criticise the status quo, but it does not take much to notice the difference between how the intellectual portrays the things she defends and how things appear on the ground. Much of the public intellectual work done on behalf of the natural sciences by both philosophers and professional scientists has this peculiar character. For example, the leading philosophical defenders of science in recent times – Karl Popper and Thomas Kuhn – were conversant in the physical sciences of their day but continually returned to achievements from the previous 50 years or earlier to ground their

philosophical defences of science. Of course, Popper and Kuhn found opposing virtues in the same history – Popper saw the testing of heroic hypotheses, while Kuhn saw peaceful puzzle-solving. Yet, despite their disagreements, both located the value of science in its capacity for autonomous inquiry. The great unspoken premise they jointly conceded was that that capacity had been compromised, if not inhibited altogether, as science had come to be more enveloped in the rest of the social order.

As for the great science popularisers, two ideal types may be identified. On the one hand, there is the accomplished physicist, now retired from active research (e.g. the Nobel-Prize-winning Steven Weinberg); on the other, the biologist who, despite an élite pedigree, left the research arena early to become a full-time populariser (e.g. Oxford's Professor of Public Understanding of Science, Richard Dawkins). Common to both types of populariser is a vision of all science – not merely their own science – as much more unified than the full range of activities that regularly pass as 'scientific' research would suggest. (The word 'reductionist' is sometimes used by critics to denigrate this vision.) One suspects that these popularisers do not see themselves as public relations agents or under-labourers for today's researchers, but as keeping alive a fading ideal – a unified vision of reality – in a period when actual circumstances conspire to pull science apart in many different directions. Thus, a reader inspired by such work would have a hard time locating an academic degree programme to follow up the full range of subjects digested and synthesised. Topics of recent popularisation like 'evolutionary psychology', 'memetics' or 'complexity theory' describe more a cross-disciplinary network of maverick researchers than an established scientific discipline.

In contrast, intellectuals who locate their ideals in the status quo need not be conservative. But if they are, it is in the literal sense of trying to 'conserve' something of the present that threatens to decline or disappear altogether without due attention. The threats may come from moral corruption, ideological subversion, foreign invasion, as well as the unintended consequences of quite normal forms of behaviour. The peculiar brand of paranoia associated with intellectual defences of the monarchy, the Church, tradition, culture and, most recently, 'family values' falls under this rubric. Still the most eloquent expression of this perspective is Matthew Arnold's essays collected together in 1869 as *Culture and Anarchy*. Arnold, a Victorian schools inspector, provided the first Anglophone account of the intellectual as a free-ranging cultural critic who is in an ongoing struggle to save the best in civilisation from both its decadent would-be defenders in the aristocracy ('barbarians') and its upwardly mobile levellers in the bourgeoisie ('philistines'). However, a conservative who is sanguine that the status quo will maintain itself without such strenuous efforts is probably not an intellectual – but that wouldn't disqualify her from possibly being correct.

Less obviously, the status quo may also be the source of liberal intellectual ideals. The trick involves showing that the present consummates trends that the liberal intellectual has been anticipating (and implicitly advocating) for some time. Social scientists often acquire their status as intellectuals on this basis. It requires a strong dose of what I earlier called Whig history. However, it is never clear whether these intellectuals have achieved genuine feats of social prediction or merely reinterpreted their originally vague hypotheses so as to confer legitimacy on the current power-holders. Because the latter is often suspected, these intellectuals may ultimately suffer harsh treatment by the bulk of social scientists who are still rewarded more by their colleagues than by outside sources of money and influence. (Indeed, a positive indicator of academic solidarity is that these intellectuals are seen as 'tainted'.) The result may be strong recognition in policy circles in one's lifetime without leaving a strong academic trace upon retirement. A striking example is the sociologist Daniel Bell who was responsible for two phrases – and an attendant body of theorising – that defined and justified the horizons of US public policy over the last four decades: 'the end of ideology' and 'post-industrial society'. However, despite having held distinguished chairs at Columbia and Harvard, Bell has been largely written out of the history of sociology.

Of course, the fate of the liberal who defends the status quo may not be so drastic. The intellectual's situation may be improved if she also exerts significant control over the means of knowledge production, such as ownership of a key publishing house. This bare fact serves as a warning that incisive criticism of the intellectual's activities will be met not with a vigorous public response but with a more covert restriction of the critic's future publication opportunities. Such veiled threats may enable the intellectual's courtier functions to pass with little explicit criticism, and even a modicum of respect from the larger social science community. As a result, the intellectual's reputation may linger a bit longer than Bell's has. A case to watch here is Anthony Giddens, Britain's leading sociology textbook writer who in the 1990s metamorphosed into the mastermind behind Tony Blair's 'Third Way' between socialism and neo-liberalism. Along the way, Giddens co-founded Polity Press, which now publishes a substantial chunk of all social theory books in English, including translations of recent works from continental Europe.

How should intellectuals engage with politicians?

Intellectuals are practitioners of the politics of time with posterity as their constituency. Their natural role is that of balancing the ledger, revealing that any advantage is always temporary and reversible. This means, on general matters of politics, intellectuals should aim their fire at the strong but not the weak: either the strong should be cut down or the weak built up. In sum, an intellectual can be a *demystifier* or a *sophist*. 'Authoritarian regimes' – an expression that should be interpreted broadly to cover all forms of clearly marked authority including scientific expertise – demand demystification. In liberal regimes, where power differences are not so explicitly marked, intellectuals function better as sophists who help to boost arguments that are not so much prohibited as 'unpopular' or otherwise unsupported by the usual informal market mechanisms through which ideas are exchanged.

Politicians pose some special challenges to intellectuals in liberal democracies, which officially respect the spirit of autonomy and free inquiry for which the intellectual stands. Here the politician is likely to appear as Mephistopheles in Goethe's *Faust*: someone who will exploit your vices in the name of extolling your virtues. Intellectuals should be especially wary of two types of political injunctions that invite her collusion:

1. 'We need an open public discussion before making policy!'
2. 'We need more research before making policy!'

Both injunctions trade on the indisputable relevance of knowledge to action. However, no amount of knowledge can ever replace the *decision* that must be eventually taken to license action. This decision is epitomised by a couple of questions: How are we to organise this knowledge, giving each bit its due weight? When have we got enough knowledge to take action?

Ultimately a decision requires that the decision-maker take responsibility for an outcome over which she is unlikely to have full control. However, 'responsibility' is a scary word for politicians because it implies exposure to error and blame, should the decision not turn out as desired. This prospect can have devastating consequences at election time. Thus, politicians are always tempted to offload or defer decisions in ways that allow them to escape any potential fallout. The two injunctions highlighted above suggest two strategies for politicians to evade responsibility.

In the case of (1), politicians devise multiple means of eliciting public opinion on some issue, say, the procedure for disposing of nuclear waste. These may range from telephone and internet polls to focus groups and consensus conferences. However, as any social scientist knows, public opinion elicited by such vastly different means is likely to produce contradictory results. Different sorts of people tend to voice their opinions by the different means, which in turn allow them to engage with the issue in significantly different ways. The overall result leaves the politicians with virtually complete discretion over what to do, since at least one of these commissioned vehicles of public opinion is bound to support whatever decision the politicians ultimately take. Thus, the politicians need not bear the full responsibility for their decision; rather they can offload it to the most expedient indicator of the popular will.

When politicians can exert greater control over when a decision is taken, the case of (2) is more appropriate. Here politicians can capitalise on the endless ingenuity displayed by scientists – both natural and social – in adapting their research agendas to suit the needs of potential clients, so as to feed their own endless need for funds. Moreover, the natural tendency of scientists to want to examine things more comprehensively, in greater detail and, of course, with an eye towards a renewal of their contract, nicely plays into politicians' own propensity to temporise, whenever possible. Never have the worst character traits of two groups worked to such mutual advantage.

How should intellectuals engage with academics in general?

Academics have a long and tortured relationship with intellectuals. Although they should be on the same side, if not the same people, academics and intellectuals usually regard each other with mutual suspicion. Each treats the other as an interloper who floods the market with inferior products. Most of what passes for 'criticism' in academia strikes the true intellectual as little more than *comfort thinking*, whereby criticism is cloaked in an esoteric jargon that amuses one's colleagues but goes over the head of its putative target and hence merely succeeds in comforting the converted. The intellectual is less interested in sharing inside jokes than in ensuring that the target has felt her sting and, ideally, changed her mind.

However, academics are probably more suspicious of intellectuals, including those who began life as academics, than vice versa. To academics, intellectuals appear impressionistic in their observations, biased in their judgements, sloppy in their research, and parasitic on the work of others – typically other academics. Note the mixed motives at work here. Academics appear to be worried about at least three things: receiving due credit for their work, protecting their work from debasement and, most subtly, justifying the very need for their work. The last worry concedes that intellectuals at their best can reduce complex academic arguments to their key points and then provide a context for them that conveys a significance that attracts a much wider audience than academics normally manage.

The intellectual's dual mastery of distillation and amplification raises the question of why academics feel they must engage in laborious data gathering embellished with great swathes of jargon. To the naïve observer, academic activity looks like an increasingly ostentatious display of authority, especially as costs mount not only for gathering the data but even for acquiring the relevant jargon-wielding skills. Yet the results seem to offer a meagre advance on already established lines of thought. Academic texts are usually more interesting for their footnotes than their main argument – that is, for what they consume than what they produce. Most academic work only adds some focus to things that have been already observed, rarely revealing genuinely new vistas. This is why intellectuals can often usurp the public authority of academics simply by providing a broader context for the latest research finding.

Academics try to discourage intellectuals from spanning several fields by pointing to the rapidly expanding and advancing research frontier, starting in the physical sciences but increasingly mimicked by other academic fields. Accordingly, a would-be 'universal intellectual' must yield to competent specialists who know when to assert and when to defer. Yet this frequently heard judgement should not quite ring true with journalists who have had to study up quickly on some specialised research topic. The bigger problem is always the second-order one of where to turn to find the relevant background knowledge for making sense of a putatively new finding. However, once that problem is solved, the significance of the discovery itself falls into place quite easily.

That contemporary academia seems to consist of largely self-contained and disconnected specialities may be simply an artefact of poor pedagogy at the more advanced levels of training. When training occurs mainly with an eye to placing students at the cutting edge of research, the relevant intellectual background is provided only on a need-to-know basis, leaving students with a spotty and misleading understanding of how the research frontier came to be as it is. Scientists in particular are trained so as to have an intrinsic interest *only* in working on a set of problems because they are not provided with an opportunity to nurture the broader reasons why, say, an intellectual might be interested in a line of inquiry. Were the development of a speciality presented in a straightforwardly historical fashion, it would become easier to see the intellectual motivation for the current crop of technical problems, as well as their considerable overlap with the problems tackled by neighbouring fields.

So, are there any good reasons for academics trying to outlaw universal intellectuals? There is a superficially persuasive banality: that more people continue to be involved in research, which leads to the production of more books and articles. Yet, at the same time, these people and their work are not treated equally by academics. Most of the attention is focused on relatively few authors and texts. So academic appeals to the sheer magnitude of their enterprise ultimately backfire, since even academics seem to have ways of getting around it. The intellectual is then presented with the opportunity to query why so many people should enter academia to do research that few people – including other academics – will bother to take seriously. In this respect, the field of library and information science should be a breeding ground for intellectuals critical of business as usual in academia.

At a deeper level, the academic's jibe against the prospects of a universal intellectual reeks of what the political economist Albert Hirschman has called *the rhetoric of reaction*. Reactionary rhetoric denies the possibility of universal progress on the grounds that the world's complexity ultimately transcends human comprehension. This was the main objection to the Enlightenment in the 18th and early 19th centuries. It was often made by religious thinkers who believed that in the name of science the Enlightenment sacrilegiously attributed to the human what could be predicated only of the divine. In the 20th century, this argument reappeared in secular guise, thanks to Austrian economists, especially Friedrich Hayek. It is now the standard neo-liberal objection to the meliorative claims made on behalf of state-based socialism: no central planner could ever reproduce, let alone improve upon, the intelligence distributed among agents intimately familiar with the local environments in which they normally operate. Better then to let the agents go about their business unimpeded, interacting when necessary, allowing the invisible hand to work in its mysteriously 'emergent' ways.

However, as Hirschman observes, only a universal intellectual – perhaps the very last one or one to whom God has given special dispensation – could pronounce on the *ultimacy* of a central planner's ignorance. After all, if even the central planner is indeed no more than one among many dispersed agents with a fragmentary grasp of the whole field of action, how could she ever be *certain* that her plans for progress towards a universal norm will turn out to be futile? Such negative certainty seems to imply the knowledge of outcomes that our finitude denies by definition. If we cannot be sure that we shall achieve all to which our thoughts and actions aspire, it also follows that we cannot be sure that we shall *not* achieve it. Logic can provide a counsel of hope as well as resignation in matters of intellectual policy.

How should intellectuals deal with scientists, more specifically?

Scientists are the trickiest adversaries for intellectuals to handle in a public setting. To be sure, the discerning public recognises science's chequered track record. Nevertheless, scientists usually have no trouble displaying their achievements and the overall good of their activities. Moreover, scientists are presumed expert in at least the areas where they claim dominion, and typically more. All of these features, which speak to the scientist's prima facie credibility, place the intellectual at a distinct disadvantage.

Scientists often try to pre-empt intellectual debate altogether by appealing to *facts*, as in, 'If you really knew the facts, we wouldn't be having this debate'. Here the scientist tries to undermine your equal footing by turning the encounter into a tutorial. In that case, you must repay the compliment by becoming the inquisitive student. After all, appeals to facts are rarely just about facts but also about the theoretical language used to describe and explain them. Indeed, a fact often conceals more baggage than the public may wish to carry or even handle. So, when a scientist asserts, say, that intelligence is 60 per cent inherited, you should ask how the fact's key terms are empirically specified, or 'operationalised'. No doubt the scientist will respond that her operational-isations conform to standard practice in her field, which defines, say, 'intelligence' in terms of what is registered on standardised aptitude tests. But of course, the relevant question is whether the public – not the scientist's colleagues – should take this fact on board. It is the intellectual's job to ensure that the two questions are not confused.

Here you might query how the facts would look had the key terms been operationalised somewhat differ-ently, perhaps to reflect a more ordinary understanding of the key terms in the fact. This would then allow you to highlight the rather contingent – perhaps even arbitrary – relationship between the purported topic of investi-gation and the scientific means used to address it. One would hate to think that public interest has been held hostage by a quirk in the history of science.

This point is of larger relevance to the intellectual's dealings with scientists. The advertised strength of scientific research is its *reliability*, which means that the results stand up after repeated testing. In fields requiring significant technical competence, scientists can easily agree on what counts as reliable research. Reliability shows that scientists are good at what they do. What reliability does not show is that scientists are good at what needs to be done. This pertains to the *validity* of their research, something much harder to determine. For example, biomedical scientists may reliably show that cancer in rats injected with a certain drug goes into remission, but it does not follow that the scientists have found a cure for cancer in humans. Similarly, social scientists may reliably show that a certain policy lowers street crime in poor US neighbourhoods without thereby having demonstrated that the policy would work in similar neighbourhoods in the UK.

The question of validity turns on the generalisability of the research: can you get the same results when and where it counts? The hope of an affirmative answer drives the public perception of science as an engine of social progress. Of course, the hope is sometimes fulfilled but often it is not. Nevertheless, as scientists struggle to keep their research programmes solvent, they sometimes permit their findings to bask in an undeserved glow of validity. Here the intellectual should follow the trail of money and power that attends this drift from reliability to validity, science's own great 'bait-and-switch'. The scientists' implicit pitch may go something like this: 'We promise (say) a cure for cancer in humans but in fact we plan to study cancer in other animals for a bit longer because that's what we really know how to do well.'

Generally speaking, the validity of a line of research can be questioned if it claims to have – almost – solved a complex problem by using a single method or research design. Scientists who feel compelled to make such claims simply reflect the highly competitive environment for research funding, which encourages rivals to stress their differences and otherwise raise barriers to intellectual free trade.

When sizing up scientists, intellectuals should adapt for their purposes a sly remark by one of the great Austrian intellectuals, the journalist Karl Kraus. Kraus said that psychoanalysis is the disease of which it claims to be the cure. Scientists go one better: they take the raw material of everyday life and manufacture problems only they can then solve. A slightly caricatured example drives home the point. You notice over the years that you do not need to wear an overcoat so often in the winter. You adapt accordingly and even welcome the slight rise in temperatures – that is, until a climatologist informs you that this change is part of an overall warming of the planet that will lead to global catastrophe unless you significantly change your lifestyle. In believing the climatologist, you effectively cede sovereignty over matters for which you had previously taken personal responsibility. We are most used to this increasing sense of epistemic dependency from medicine, so that most people nowadays believe that their general practitioner knows more about their body than they do.

That Machiavelli of science, the French sociologist Bruno Latour, celebrates this subtlest form of authoritarianism. According to Latour, the astute scientist leverages the laboratory into a principle of governance that avoids the normally contested political channels of coercion and election. Not surprisingly, his hero turns out to be Louis Pasteur, whose experimental findings in medicine, agriculture and industry transformed French society more thoroughly and peacefully than the manoeuvres of the cleverest politicians in the nation's history. In the case of Pasteur – as well as those of the climatologist and the general medical practitioner – the question of the ends justifying the means looms large, at least to the intellectual: is the benefit you receive worth the loss of intellectual autonomy that comes from ceding your right to contest, to question – and perhaps even to be wrong?

How should intellectuals deal with philosophers?

Generally speaking, philosophers secure their intellectual authority by turning every substantive dispute into a logically prior dispute about the meaning of some key evaluative word, such as 'true' or 'good'. The two main contemporary schools, analytic and continental philosophers, have their own characteristic ways of executing this strategy. Analytic philosophers tend to say that all substantive disagreements over the truth presuppose some common conception of truth. On the contrary, claim continental philosophers, even truths that command the widest assent betray a multiplicity of underlying conceptions of what it is to be true. Needless to say, together the two schools cancel out each other.

Moreover, in both cases it is clear that the philosophers lack a clear substantive view of their own about what actually is true. You can reveal this weak flank by granting the philosopher's definition of a pet term like 'true' and then showing how your own substantive position satisfies that definition. If you do this right, then the most the philosopher can say in response is that positions opposed to your own also satisfy the definition. You are then free to ask why, in that case, the philosopher wishes to insist on a definition at all.

An opinionated philosopher may try to 'stoop' to your level and defend a substantive thesis counter to your own. But make sure she doesn't have it both ways. If the (probably analytic) philosopher has previously offered a definition, then accuse her of special pleading on behalf of the particular spin she gives to it. Definitions of freedom that imply the superiority of market economies or definitions of progress that coincide with the latest developments in the natural sciences are fair game here. If, on the other hand, the (probably continental) philosopher has claimed that all such definitions are arbitrary, then your command over the empirical features of your own position should suffice to rebuff her challenge. So, if the philosopher tries to cast you as a metaphysical reprobate who still believes in the existence of class- or gender-based oppression when sophisticated philosophy has 'de-essentialised' such 'signifiers', you can accuse her of having merely prohibited words but not eliminated the corresponding activities – except perhaps in the élite circles in which she normally travels.

Philosophy's insubstantiality is a by-product of the peculiar way philosophers strive for a universalist perspective. They are control freaks – but only at the level of language. Whereas intellectuals normally get into the trenches with their interlocutors, work with their starting positions, and then subject their own claims to the opponent's scrutiny, philosophers don't function well unless they are in full control of the terms of the argument. This means repackaging the interlocutor's position in a form that then enables the philosopher to deploy the same set of tricks she uses on all arguments. Analytic philosophers call their set of tricks 'logic', whereas continental philosophers defer to the authority of the master in whose name they speak, as in the omnipresent possibility of a 'Freudian gloss' of whatever the interlocutor happens to say.

Why do intellectuals seem to thrive on conflict?

Intellectuals thrive on conflict for reasons relating to both their ends and means. Intellectuals seek the whole truth, which pre-commits them to getting the opponent on board. It follows that any difference of opinion is a conflict waiting to happen, the avoidance of which always straddles the fine line between diplomacy and cowardice. Truth in this singular and universal sense can be achieved only through *dialectics*. Dialectics works by forcing someone who asserts a thesis to defend herself against someone else who believes the same evidence can be used to support a contradictory or even a contrary thesis. Logicians today trivialise this strategy of generating opposition without adding to the common body of evidence as a mere 'shift in the burden of proof'. But to an intellectual, logicians invest too much in the durability of the things we take for granted and too little in the sheer contingency that those things are the ones that are durable. Here intellectuals can take comfort in the judgement of historians, who generally regard the formalisation of the dialectical method by the greatest intellectual of the Middle Ages, Peter Abelard, as the first tentative step towards the modern era.

The fruits of dialectical inquiry can be fully realised only in the rare 'open societies' – to use Karl Popper's term – that welcome dissent because their members are confident that it will strengthen society in the long term. A good test of a society's openness is the extent to which institutional reproduction is rendered game-like, as in the case of periodic elections for public office. The idea here – one very dear to the sophists – is that any track record is always a matter of contingency that can be potentially overturned, provided the right opportunity. The value of periodically starting with a clean slate or levelled playing field is not that it returns to a pristine state of nature, but rather that it forces society as it currently is to decide whether to carry on or change course. Normal societies, however, exist more fearfully in varying states of intellectual closure, whereby disagreeable opinions appear in a silenced or distorted form, and elections are kept to the bare minimum, certainly in terms of the overall impact.

Conflict is central to the basic mode of intellectual life, *criticism*. Criticism involves the formation of a judgement towards something that the critic believes could – and typically should – have been otherwise. Thus, criticism sharply distinguishes between 'subject' (the critic) and 'object' (the criticised) yet also implies that the subject has an interest in the object even though she may have had nothing to do with its construction. The negative connotations attached to the Yiddish 'kibitzer' and the English 'backseat driver' reveal that the critic's role is not especially endearing. So then why have intellectuals made criticism central to their identity? The short answer is that criticism is precisely what the highly fallible *Homo sapiens* deserves, a point that, of course, applies no less to the intellectual. The cost of acquiring any knowledge at all is that it will be biased by the conditions surrounding its acquisition. It is just this bias that the intellectual exposes to criticism in the hope that a perspective of wider validity might result – at least one to which both the critic and the criticised could give assent.

Voltaire was unique in acknowledging the dignity of criticism as a form of human conflict. He keenly defended the rights of his opponents to criticise him, even when he could have had them censored, while he was always wary of self-avowed allies who suppressed their criticisms of him so as not to cause offence. Both attitudes reveal a calling higher than the mere promotion or preservation of self-interest. To uphold the dignity of criticism both protects the integrity of ideas and shows respect to the person conveying them. It might even be said that intellectuals are inherently self-destructive: they help to generate their own competition by advocating mass education, newspaper reading and public debate. Thus, intellectuals encourage others to follow their deed rather than their word in a particular sense: better someone criticise what I say than repeat what I say uncritically. This may also explain how intellectuals most differ from the likes of academics, entrepreneurs and politicians. They don't mind being shown they're wrong, as long as they are credited with the right mistakes and permitted to make more in the future. This is how best to understand a maxim often cynically attributed to intellectuals: 'There is no such thing as bad publicity, but being ignored is tantamount to death.'

Why aren't intellectuals ever truly appreciated? What can be done about that?

Criticism is rarely received as a gift, especially when delivered by intellectuals. They tend to target not single ideas or propositions but entire bodies of thought that, in the heat of polemic, are easily confused with their bearers. Thus, an intellectual's criticism is often taken personally. In revenge, intellectuals then become the messengers killed for their messages. You are never formally refuted – you are simply *repossessed*. Indeed, you know you're an intellectual when people denounce you in speech and plagiarise you in writing. However, precisely because you're an intellectual, you are in no position to complain about this fate. As the fearless defender of the free movement of ideas, you could hardly wish your valuable ideas to be permanently associated with the mortal coil from which they sprang.

Instead you may take comfort in having injected the vaccine that immunises the body politic against still more virulent ideas. This was the role to which Desiderius Erasmus, the great Renaissance Humanist, aspired, when he tried to bridge the gulf between the Catholic Church and the emerging Protestant dissenters in the early 16th century. Admittedly the role is not for the squeamish. Its open-minded reasonableness becomes more visible the farther away one stands from the field of conflict. Based on a close textual reading of the Bible in its ancient languages, Erasmus concluded that *none* of the divisive claims made by the Catholics (e.g. papal infallibility) and the Protestants (e.g. pre-destination) could be justified. Of course, some of these claims may be justifiable in terms of contemporary problems relating to Church corruption. However, Erasmus insisted that they be treated as purely secular issues without the metaphysical mystification to which all sides were prone.

While Erasmus certainly enjoyed notoriety in his lifetime and had direct access to both Catholic and Protestant leaders, his work failed to pre-empt the Reformation but may have ultimately helped to justify the peaceful coexistence of multiple Christian denominations *after* the Reformation. In his day, however, Erasmus was a suspicious character. All sides wondered which side he was 'really' on. This problem of self-presentation highlights an expertise intellectuals typically arrogate to themselves as critics-at-large: they claim the ability to separate the wheat from the chaff in contested knowledge claims so that all may benefit. Unfortunately, what the intellectual designates as 'chaff' all too often corresponds to features that a group regards as essential to its identity, *especially* in times of conflict. Only after some time has passed and the combatants have left the field does the intellectual's conceptual surgery come to be appreciated. Thus, by the dawn of the Enlightenment, when the major religious wars had ended, Erasmus had come to be seen as an icon of tolerance and an inspiration for the further secularisation of theology.

Scientists have developed an attractive strategy for managing the *problem of repossession*: how can the intellectual absorb criticism of what she said yet retain credit for what she meant? The strategy offers an answer to those who wonder why science today is not more 'heroic': why are there no more Galileos? Galileo was an exception among scientists in fully embracing the role of the intellectual. He took personal responsibility for his ideas by explicitly contradicting Church authority. Upon his death, Galileo was celebrated – at least in more intellectually progressive circles – as a unique personality with a distinctive style of reasoning. But his substantive contribution to science became secure only once his ideas and observations were incorporated within Newtonian mechanics. Galileo himself never founded a school or designed a research programme for others to finish. He tried to do it all himself. Galileo had sufficient confidence – even as he acknowledged his fallibilities – to take on tasks that would now be delegated to several people, perhaps across several generations.

A much more common pattern in science has been for radical theorists to retain possession of their theories by dividing the labour of the intellectual. Thus, the brunt of controversy is borne by the theorist's agents. Galileo the public advocate, Galileo the innovative theorist and Galileo the reliable observer would thus become at least three people. Isaac Newton, the originator of the most influential theory in the history of science, consciously recruited supporters who conjured up a 'Newtonian' movement in both science and the larger society. For example, Newton realised that the formidable mathematical structure of his physics would probably turn off many potential readers and make others suspicious of the metaphysical assumptions hidden in his many proofs. Thus, he trained largely innumerate intellectuals in theology and the wider public culture to fight for the Newtonian cause in more general terms that enabled the theory to be compared and contrasted with the other leading natural philosophies of the day. The glosses written by one of these recruits, the political theorist John Locke, ended up influencing Enlightenment *philosophes* like Voltaire whose intellectual centre of gravity was in the humanities.

Combatants in today's 'Science Wars' could learn a few things from how Newtonian mechanics acquired its standing among 18th-century intellectuals, a status that lasted until the early 20th century. The phrase 'Science Wars' was coined by the Anglo-American cultural critic Andrew Ross to capture science's struggle for legitimacy in the post-Cold-War era, a period marked by both the withdrawal of state support for science and the rise in citizen and consumer interest in science's impact on society. However, these larger changes were quickly reduced to an academic dispute focused on the question: how much science does one need to know to comment sensibly on it? The climax of the academic infighting was a book co-authored by two physicists, Alan Sokal and Jean Bricmont, published in the US in 1998 under the title *Fashionable Nonsense*. There Sokal and Bricmont detailed various errors and misunderstandings committed by contemporary French intellectuals influential in the Anglophone world who try to use cutting-edge science as a basis for cultural criticism.

Were Newton teleported to the theatre of the Science Wars, he would immediately spot the problem. In a time when science clearly needs to justify its existence, shouldn't the strategy be to build bridges rather than draw boundaries? Given the spontaneous enthusiasm of these French intellectuals (and their admirers) for the latest developments in science, why not use that as an opportunity to instruct them in what could easily become a gospel to be spread in the larger society? After all, the radical conclusions of these intellectuals appear to be based on faulty understandings of science that they *endorse*. The best strategy, then, is not to deride them or, worse, prohibit them from associating science with larger cultural trends. Rather, it should be to provide them with a level of scientific knowledge sufficient to the task. Of course, this strategy would force scientists to think about science as intellectuals normally do – not as an inviolate body of knowledge, but as a message that can be adapted to many media. One area of contemporary science that appears to have benefited from Newton's example is the latest incarnation of Social Darwinism known as 'evolutionary psychology', which probably exists more robustly in popular books, articles and websites (especially www.edge.org) than on university campuses.

A crucial feature of the Newton-Darwin strategy is that, unlike Galileo, the scientific principals try to remain studiously above the frays associated with their names. This makes it easier for their theories to be discussed in an open, even heated, fashion without worrying about causing personal offence to their originators. In this environment, the discussants typically absorb the blame – as 'bad defenders' – while credit reverts to the originator of the theory discussed. To be sure, Newton, who obsessed about his originality, only partly followed his own advice. Life became much easier for his followers upon his death. They then enjoyed the freedom to take 'Newtonianism' in directions that the master neither anticipated nor perhaps would have fully approved.

In contrast, Darwin's sickly disposition provides a clearer case of an intellectual who consistently argued by proxy, benefiting from both ideological opportunists like Herbert Spencer, whose theory of evolution pre-dated and significantly deviated from Darwin's, and Pauline converts like Thomas Henry Huxley, who saw Darwin's theory as demanding a post-theological redefinition of humanity. The professionalisation of science in the 20th century has made it easier for intellectual arguments to be conducted by proxy. Indeed, the success of Albert Einstein, originally a Swiss patent officer, is largely due to the mediation of Max Planck, himself a founder of quantum mechanics and the editor of Germany's leading physics journal. Planck, an enterprising academic 'gatekeeper', was on the lookout for new ideas and did what was necessary to present them in a form that would force colleagues to take them seriously.

What is the toughest challenge facing the intellectual?
There are many candidates for this title. Each challenge involves cutting across the fixed categories normally used to organise people: appeals for cross-class, cross-gender

or cross-ethnic coalitions spring to mind. However, the toughest challenge is *cross-generational.* The challenge of communicating ideas across age groups will remain even after enlightened polities have equitably redistributed incomes, blurred sexual identities and mixed races. This is simply because there is no clever way of redistributing, blurring or mixing attitudes that are primarily the result of temporal differences – that people live when they do in history. Perhaps time-travel could address this problem, though it has yet to figure credibly in any intellectual's arsenal.

Consider some conflicting cross-generational tendencies that interfere with an intellectual's ability to convey her message. The old may be in power now, but the young are more likely to carry forward a new vision. The old are better placed to appreciate your comprehensive grasp of a situation, while at the same time also less motivated to grant its validity since the problems you raise have transpired on their watch. In contrast, the young may be more open-minded to new ideas, but are also less informed by what came before them, and so more likely to be puzzled by the sense of urgency you bring to issues. On the one hand, to vindicate decisions they've taken, the old may marginalise you by claiming that things, bad as they are, could not have been better. On the other hand, to keep their options open, the young may equally marginalise you by claiming that your vision of doom may not turn out so bad. In both cases, your advice goes unheeded.

A striking contemporary site for such cross-generational interference is the softening of attitudes towards the use of biological categories to explain social life. In the last quarter-century, 'eugenics' and 'socio-biology' have been effectively repackaged as 'biotech-nology' and 'evolutionary psychology' for a younger generation prone to see opportunities where their forebears could perceive only threats. The disastrous Nazi and Soviet precedents for using biomedical science as an instrument of social policy are clearly receding from collective memory. In a world where totalitarian-ism is no longer a live option, it has become possible to revisit the old biologistic perspectives – now enhanced by the latest scientific research – without the scary old political baggage. Ironically, notwithstanding the efforts of Steven Pinker and his fellow evolutionary psych-ologists, the one 'blank slate' that never seems to go away is the one responsible for their own success – namely, the blank slate of young minds born without the experience of previous generations.

The rhetorical challenge facing the intellectual, then, is to assert a critical perspective without appearing alarmist or even reactionary. Here you might try to conjure up a moment of mutual recognition between the old and the young. You could play on the fact that the old used to be young and the young will eventually become old. However, this strategy, while it may work to replenish the tax base for welfare benefits, falls short of a foolproof formula. The adaptability of the young to whatever befalls them always makes the establishment of common ground with the old a daunting task. Since a generation marches through time together, they are bound to find some kind of collectively reinforced value in whatever hand fate has dealt them.

Of course, intellectuals should try to persuade the young that things have been better and could be better in the future. But this is easier said than done, since the young tend to see the old, not as having adopted positions suited to their times, but as having committed avoidable errors that the young now endeavour to correct. Perhaps such an illusion is necessary to keep up the appearance that one is always making progress. What the young fail to appreciate, however, is that the errors made by their elders were – and always will be – unavoidable precisely because the errors were suited, as will be the young's, to their times. Reminding each generation of this basic point means that the intellectual need not worry that her services might become obsolete. At the same time, it suggests that the perseverance of a Sisyphus is required to provide these services.

Consider someone born after 1970, virtually any-where in the world. What does *socialism* mean to such a person? It means the dismantling of the Soviet Union and the replacement of bloated welfare states with lean-and-mean neo-liberal regimes. To this person socialism looks like a failed social experiment that, taken to its logical conclusion, became, in Ronald Reagan's phrase, an 'evil empire'. The fall of the Berlin Wall in 1989 erased a century's worth of achievements done either explicitly to promote socialism or covertly to steal the socialists' thunder. These include industrial development and the regularisation of employment, the redistribution of personal and corporate income, the universal provision of healthcare and education and the redressing of traditional class-, race- and gender-based forms of discrimination. However, to someone born after 1970, this larger historical trajectory is irrelevant. She thinks in terms of her lifetime, which has witnessed diminishing returns on such socialist-inspired investments. It has cost the taxpayer more and more to achieve less and less, and there has even been backsliding on some of the old targets – as the gap between the rich and the poor starts to widen again.

Perhaps, so the younger generation concludes, we have reached a *real* barrier. Moreover, the reality of this barrier may be so deep that a radical rethinking of politics is required. To the intellectual with the audacity to view things *sub specie aeternitatis* ('under the guise of eternity'), the number of generations that have bestridden the planet makes it very unlikely that an extreme judgement of this kind is *ever* warranted. Nevertheless, it serves to flatter the cohort of each new generation, who wish to believe that they live in uniquely revolutionary times. (The irony – for those who speak God's official language – is that 'revolution' means 'return' in Latin.) No one has more exploited this bias in the young than that great theorist of animal liberation, Peter Singer, perhaps the most influential professional philosopher in the public sphere today.

Singer has called for the replacement of Marx with Darwin as the intellectual firmament of leftist politics. However, Singer's is a decidedly post-socialist left with the sort of scaled-down policy expectations suitable to our neo-liberal times. Given the causal primacy afforded to sexual reproduction in Darwin's theory of evolution, the following argument should send shivers up feminist spines: 'While Darwinian thought has no impact on the priority we give to equality as a moral or political ideal, it gives us grounds for believing that since men and women play different roles in reproduction, they may also differ in their inclinations and temperaments, in ways that best promote the reproductive prospects of each sex' (*A Darwinian Left*, pp. 17–18). Singer says this might explain why still so few women manage to reach the top of their fields and why the difference between men's and women's salaries remains significant, despite several decades of corrective legislation. He does not consider the intellectually less outré but politically more controversial possibility that the remaining 'gender gaps' would be eventually closed by persisting with refined versions of the same strategies that have been used up to this point.

Singer's influence adumbrates a major shift in political strategy that intellectuals ignore at their peril. An article of faith for intellectuals of the Enlightenment was that scientific progress is the motor of social progress, where 'social progress' means maximising the welfare of humanity. The major political disagreements of the last 200 years can be understood as having been about tactics, especially whether equality among individual humans is necessary to realise the overall goal. However, the disenchantment of the younger generation with conventional politics suggests that something has indeed changed. The belief in scientific progress as the motor of social progress remains, but the major terms of the belief have been subject to diminished expectations.

First, humans are neither the sole nor even the privileged members of society. Second, science is understood more as the bearer of brute facts than as the inspiration for transcendent technologies. These two shifts justify a tendency to attribute value to a wider variety of things but less value to each such thing. Thus, as humans and animals form part of the same moral economy, it is becoming increasingly reasonable to save very healthy animals from 'torture' in laboratory experiments, even if that means very sick humans must die. It would seem that some default standard of 'natural law' is re-emerging as a measure of political judgement. The burden of proof is shifting to those who would counteract spontaneous tendencies with deliberate artifice. However, the intellectual should hold her ground in support of artifice. What is presented by the likes of Singer as an intellectually more expansive point of view is really an admission of political defeat and quite possibly a rationalisation for a loss of nerve in the uphill struggle to become fully human.

* * *

The intellectual is the eternal irritant: the grit in the oyster out of which humanity will hopefully emerge as a pearl.

POSTSCRIPT: WHAT
BECOMES OF INTELLECTUALS
WHEN THEY DIE?

The year 2005 marks the centenary of the birth of two of the profoundest intellectuals of the Cold War era, Jean-Paul Sartre and Raymond Aron. Their tense 50-year acquaintance began with a shared élite French education that included a formative period in Germany just before the rise of Nazism. There Aron discovered Max Weber's sociology, and Sartre studied Edmund Husserl's phenomenology. In maturity, both enjoyed a popular audience for at least a quarter of a century – Sartre by his best-selling novels and plays, Aron by his lectures at the Sorbonne and regular columns in *Le Figaro* and *L'Express*.

Each in his inimitable way displayed the contrariness both loved and loathed in intellectuals: Aron fancied Anglo-American liberalism before it became fashionable, while Sartre remained a Communist sympathiser after the fashion had passed. Aron wrote icy cool prose about the most heated geopolitical conflicts, while Sartre could turn any triviality into an existential crisis. Yet, they often stood together against the French political establishment. Both joined the Resistance when France was a Nazi puppet state, and both called for Algerian independence once France was returned to sovereignty.

Unfortunately, Sartre and Aron are also joined in death. Both have been disowned, ignored or underrated by all the academic disciplines – philosophy, literature, sociology, politics – to which their voluminous works might be thought to have contributed. Moreover, theirs is a fate perennially suffered by intellectuals. But why?

A deep answer would stress the commitment of intellectuals to the essentially *public* character of humanity. They oppose what in the monotheistic traditions is called 'gnosticism' – the idea that human salvation requires a complete renunciation of the secular condition. In its manic phase, gnosticism licenses a 'revolution of the saints' that would liberate the spirit by destroying all existing institutions. In its depressive phase, gnosticism counsels a withdrawal from the world for the sake of preserving an élite truth always threatened with corruption by the powers that be. Academics typically find it difficult to navigate the politicised waters of intellectual life because they relate to the world as gnostics.

A more superficial answer is that intellectuals routinely commit a cardinal sin of academic life. They refuse to detach their thoughts from their times, or indeed their lives. Thus, instead of trying to achieve, however imperfectly, a timeless perspective on a well-defined patch of reality, Sartre and Aron were prompted by current events to develop a distinctive point of view on all of reality, which they repeatedly revisited and revised as the times changed. Like all true intellectuals, Sartre and Aron realised – if not advertised – that their conscience was the most reliable instrument of inquiry at their disposal.

Silenced by death, Sartre and Aron are remembered more for the attitudes they brought to whatever they wrote about than what they actually said. This comment seems to damn only because the life of the mind is no longer seen as a vehicle for moral improvement, or what in a more religious time would have been called 'soul crafting'.

When Sartre and Aron did research that looked more like scholarship than journalism, they refused to disappear into their subjects. They chose subjects who provoked in them feelings of ambivalence, antagonism and even contempt. They cultivated emotions that compelled an acknowledgement of the differences between themselves and another. Not surprisingly, Aron's studies of Marx and Sartre's of Flaubert end up saying more about their authors than their subjects. But is there anything wrong with that?

Something indeed would be wrong if, as most academics believe, an ideal account of Marx or Flaubert should limit itself to presenting him as he was understood in his day – including, of course, the deeper social, economic and political factors that influenced his reception. However, if we should also have to explain *our own* interest in Marx or Flaubert, then the more explicitly reflexive presentation favoured by intellectuals like Aron and Sartre is called for.

Ironically, when academics try to recover the lived experience of historical agents, they tend to avail themselves of a narrow range of their own experience – typically only what permits empathy for the agents. To an intellectual, such trans-generational tact looks like the last vestige of ancestor worship. The refusal of academics to engage with their subjects in the full range of human emotions is an admission of defeat, be it expressed by a dignified silence or an enthusiastic endorsement. Academics may believe that they have arrived too late to turn the past towards a different future, but intellectuals are forever hopeful – and hence defiant.

FOR FURTHER READING

Theodor Adorno, *Introduction to Sociology.* Cambridge: Polity Press, 2000.

Michael Apted, *42 Up: Give Me the Child at Seven, and I Will Show You the Man.* London: New Press, 2000.

Hannah Arendt, *Eichmann in Jerusalem.* New York: Viking, 1963.

Daniel Bell, *The Coming of Post-Industrial Society.* New York: Basic Books, 1973.

Julian Benda, *The Treason of the Intellectuals* (original edn 1928). New York: Norton, 1955.

Harold Bloom, *The Anxiety of Influence.* Oxford: Oxford University Press, 1973.

Pierre Bourdieu, *Acts of Resistance: Against the New Myths of Our Times.* Cambridge: Polity Press, 1998.

Judith Butler, *Gender Trouble.* London: Routledge, 1990.

Jeremy Campbell, *The Liar's Tale: A History of Falsehood.* New York: Norton, 2001.

Edward Chancellor, *Devil Take the Hindmost: A History of Financial Speculation.* London: Macmillan, 1999.

Randall Collins, *The Sociology of Philosophies: A Global Theory of Intellectual Change.* Cambridge, MA: Harvard University Press, 1998.

Terrence Cook, *The Great Alternatives of Social Thought: Aristocrat, Saint, Capitalist, Socialist.* Lanham, MD: Rowman and Littlefield, 1991.

Richard Dawkins, *A Devil's Chaplain*. London: Weidenfeld and Nicolson, 2003.

Jonathan Dollimore, 'Bisexuality, heterosexuality, and wishful theory'. *Textual Practice*, 10: 523–39, 1996.

Barrows Dunham, *Heroes and Heretics: A Social History of Dissent*. New York: Alfred Knopf, 1963.

Jon Elster, *Sour Grapes: Studies in the Subversion of Rationality*. Cambridge: Cambridge University Press, 1983.

Michel Foucault, *Power/Knowledge: Selected Interviews and Other Writings 1972–1977*. Brighton: Harvester, 1980.

Francis Fukuyama, *The End of History and the Last Man*. New York: Free Press, 1992.

Steve Fuller, *The Governance of Science: Ideology and the Future of the Open Society*. Milton Keynes: Open University Press, 2000.

Steve Fuller, *Knowledge Management Foundations*. Woburn, MA: Butterworth-Heinemann, 2002.

Steve Fuller, *Kuhn vs Popper: The Struggle for the Soul of Science*. Cambridge: Icon Books, 2003.

Steve Fuller and James Collier, *Philosophy, Rhetoric and the End of Knowledge* (second edn; original edn 1993). Hillsdale, NJ: Lawrence Erlbaum Associates, 2004.

William Fusfield, 'To want to prove it … is … really superfluous', *Quarterly Journal of Speech*, 83: 133–51, 1997.

Ernest Gellner, *Reason and Culture*. Oxford: Blackwell, 1992.

Anthony Giddens, *The Third Way*. Cambridge: Polity Press, 1998.

John Gray, *Straw Dogs: Thoughts on Humans and Other Animals*. London: Granta, 2002.

Jürgen Habermas, *The Philosophical Discourse of Modernity*. Cambridge, MA: MIT Press, 1987.

Albert Hirschman, *The Rhetoric of Reaction*. Cambridge, MA: Harvard University Press, 1991.

Christopher Hitchens, *Letters to a Young Contrarian*. New York: Basic Books, 2001.

Ted Honderich, *After the Terror*. Edinburgh: Edinburgh University Press, 2002.

H. Stuart Hughes, *Between Commitment and Disillusion*. Middletown, CT: Wesleyan University Press, 1987.

Russell Jacoby, *The Last Intellectuals*. New York: Basic Books, 1987.

Sue Curry Jansen, *Censorship: The Knot that Binds Power and Knowledge*. Oxford: Oxford University Press, 1991.

Jeremy Jennings and Anthony Kemp-Welch, eds, *Intellectuals in Politics: From the Dreyfus Affair to Salman Rushdie*. London: Routledge, 1997.

Eliot Krause, *The Death of the Guilds: Professions, States and the Advance of Capitalism, 1930 to the Present*. New Haven, CT: Yale University Press, 1996.

Thomas Kuhn, *The Structure of Scientific Revolutions* (second edn; original edn 1970). Chicago: University of Chicago Press, 1970.

Bruno Latour, *The Pasteurization of France*. Cambridge, MA: Harvard University Press, 1988.

Mark Lilla, *The Reckless Mind: Intellectuals in Politics*. New York: New York Review of Books, 2001.

Alan Montefiore and Peter Winch, eds, *The Political Responsibility of Intellectuals*. Cambridge: Cambridge University Press, 1990.

Susan Neimann, *Evil in Modern Thought: An Alternative History of Philosophy*. Princeton, NJ: Princeton University Press, 2002.

Dick Pels, *The Intellectual as Stranger*. London: Routledge, 2001.

Steven Pinker, *The Blank Slate: The Modern Denial of Human Nature*. New York: Viking, 2002.

Karl Popper, *The Open Society and Its Enemies*. London: Routledge and Kegan Paul, 1945.

John Poulakos, *Sophistical Rhetoric in Classical Greece*. Columbia, SC: University of South Carolina Press, 1995.

Robert Proctor, *Value-Free Science? Purity and Power in Modern Knowledge*. Cambridge, MA: Harvard University Press, 1991.

Harry Redner, *Malign Masters: Gentile, Heidegger, Lukács, Wittgenstein*. London: Macmillan, 1997.

Philip Rieff, ed., *On Intellectuals*. Garden City, NY: Anchor Doubleday, 1970.

Richard Rorty, *Philosophy and Social Hope*. Harmondsworth: Penguin, 2000.

Andrew Ross, ed., *The Science Wars*. Durham, NC: Duke University Press, 1996.

Edward Said, *Representations of the Intellectual*. London: Vintage, 1994.

Salmagundi, special double issue on 'Intellectuals'. Nos 70–71 (Spring–Summer), pp. 1–352, 1986.

Ziauddin Sardar, ed., *Rescuing All Our Futures: The Future of Future Studies*. London: Adamantine Press, 1999.

Roger Shattuck, *Forbidden Knowledge: From Prometheus to Pornography*. New York: St Martin's Press, 1996.

Peter Singer, *A Darwinian Left: Politics, Evolution and Cooperation*. London: Weidenfeld and Nicolson, 1999.

Alan Sokal and Jean Bricmont, *Fashionable Nonsense*. New York: Picador, 1998.

Leo Strauss, *Persecution and the Art of Writing*. Chicago: University of Chicago Press, 1952.

Donald Swanson, 'Undiscovered Public Knowledge'. *Library Quarterly*, 56 (2): 103–18, 1986.

Eric Voegelin, *Science, Politics and Gnosticism*. Chicago: Regnery Publishing, 1968.

Steven Weinberg, *Science and Its Cultural Adversaries*. Cambridge, MA: Harvard University Press, 2001.

Bob Woodward, *Plan of Attack: The Road to War*. New York: Simon and Schuster, 2003.

Howard Zinn, *A People's History of the United States*. New York: Harper and Row, 1980.

Slavoj Žižek, *The Sublime Object of Ideology*. London: Verso, 1989.

INDEX